P9-CQD-332

Chef Recipes Made Easy

» EDITED BY DANA COWIN

FOOD&WINE

FOOD & WINE
CHEF RECIPES MADE EASY

EDITOR IN CHIEF
Dana Cowin

EDITOR
Kate Heddings

DESIGNER
Michelle Leong

SENIOR EDITOR
Colleen McKinney

ASSOCIATE WINE EDITOR
Megan Krigbaum

COPY EDITOR
Lisa Leventer

RESEARCHER
Angela McKee

DEPUTY PHOTO EDITOR
Anthony LaSala

PRODUCTION MANAGER
Matt Carson

ISBN: 978-1-932624-40-3

Published by
American Express Publishing Corporation
1120 Avenue of the Americas
New York, New York 10036

Distributed by
Charlesbridge Publishing
85 Main Street
Watertown, Massachusetts 02472

Manufactured in Canada

FOOD & WINE MAGAZINE

SVP / EDITOR IN CHIEF
Dana Cowin

CREATIVE DIRECTOR
Stephen Scoble

MANAGING EDITOR
Mary Ellen Ward

EXECUTIVE EDITOR
Pamela Kaufman

EXECUTIVE FOOD EDITOR
Tina Ujlaki

FEATURES EDITOR
Michael Endelman

ART DIRECTOR
Courtney Waddell Eckersley

**AMERICAN EXPRESS PUBLISHING
CORPORATION**

PRESIDENT / CHIEF EXECUTIVE OFFICER
Ed Kelly

CHIEF MARKETING OFFICER &
PRESIDENT, DIGITAL MEDIA
Mark V. Stanich

SVP / CHIEF FINANCIAL OFFICER
Paul B. Francis

VPs / GENERAL MANAGERS
Frank Bland, Keith Strohmeier

VP, BOOKS & PRODUCTS / PUBLISHER
Marshall Corey

DIRECTOR, BOOK PROGRAMS
Bruce Spanier

SENIOR MARKETING MANAGER,
BRANDED BOOKS
Eric Lucie

ASSISTANT MARKETING MANAGER
Stacy Mallis

DIRECTOR OF FULFILLMENT & PREMIUM VALUE
Philip Black

MANAGER OF CUSTOMER EXPERIENCE
& PRODUCT DEVELOPMENT
Charles Graver

DIRECTOR OF FINANCE
Thomas Noonan

ASSOCIATE BUSINESS MANAGER
Uma Mahabir

OPERATIONS DIRECTOR (PREPRESS)
Rosalie Abatemarco Samat

OPERATIONS DIRECTOR (MANUFACTURING)
Anthony White

FRONT COVER

PHOTOGRAPHER **Stephanie Foley**

FOOD STYLIST **Jee Levin**

PROP STYLIST **Deborah Williams**

BACK COVER FOOD PHOTOGRAPHS

SNAPPER WITH CITRUS & FENNEL SALAD
Frances Janisch

BRAISED SHORT RIBS
Lucy Schaeffer

ARUGULA SALAD WITH RICOTTA SALATA
Tina Rupp

PORK SCHNITZEL WITH POTATO SALAD
Lucy Schaeffer

BACK COVER PORTRAIT PHOTOGRAPHS

DANIEL BOULUD **Quentin Bacon**

TOM COLICCHIO **Bill Bettencourt**

LIDIA BASTIANICH **Ted Axelrod**

WOLFGANG PUCK **Amanda Marsalis**

INSIDE FLAP PORTRAIT

DANA COWIN **Mat Szwajkos**

Chef Recipes
Made Easy

» OVER 100 OF AMERICA'S FAVORITE RESTAURANT DISHES

FOOD&WINE
BOOKS

American Express Publishing Corporation, New York

Contents

chickpeas
in spicy tomato gravy
page 204

Foreword

YOU MIGHT SAY that FOOD & WINE has gumption, taking the best restaurant recipes—made with professional equipment and, sometimes, impossible-to-find ingredients—and transforming them for home cooks. But transform those recipes we did, because they're just the kind of dishes we want to eat. Editor extraordinaire Kate Heddings works to get the best recipes for the magazine's Chef Recipes Made Easy column. Then Grace Parisi, one of our Test Kitchen geniuses, reimagines those dishes. Over 100 of those reinventions are on the pages that follow. You'll find dishes like Mario Batali's lush and spicy Bucatini all'Amatriciana (we swap out the *guanciale* for easier-to-get pancetta), Tom Colicchio's incredibly tender braised short ribs (we simplify his complex cooking method) and Wolfgang Puck's crispy pork schnitzel (he uses prized Kurobuta pork; we opt for the regular kind). All told, this book is a greatest-hits collection of the most innovative thinking in food today—translated for the home cook.

Dana Cowin

Editor in Chief
FOOD & WINE Magazine

Starters &

Soups

BRUCE SHERMAN

Summer Squash & Tomato Tart

chef way

» *At North Pond in Chicago, Bruce Sherman makes individual tartlets with a variety of excellent toppings, including a spread of goat cheese and sun-dried tomato, sautéed summer squash and tomatoes and caramelized onions.*

easy way

» *Creating one large tart with premade puff pastry is a lot less work than making individual tartlets.*

» *A simple mix of prepared pesto and goat cheese tops the tart, along with sautéed squash, fresh tomato slices and green olives.*

INGREDIENTS 4 servings

- 2 tablespoons extra-virgin olive oil
- 1 pound small yellow squash, sliced ¼ inch thick
- 1 large onion, halved and thinly sliced

Salt and freshly ground white pepper

- 2 tablespoons prepared pesto
- 5 ounces fresh goat cheese, softened

All-purpose flour, for dusting

- 14 ounces puff pastry, chilled
- 1 plum tomato, very thinly sliced
- 1 large egg beaten with 2 tablespoons water
- 10 small pitted green olives, coarsely chopped

ACTIVE 30 minutes   **TOTAL** 1 hour 15 minutes

1 Preheat the oven to 425° and line a baking sheet with parchment paper. In a large skillet, heat the olive oil. Add the squash and onion and season with salt and white pepper. Cover and cook over moderately high heat, stirring occasionally, until the squash and onion are lightly browned, about 5 minutes. Remove the skillet from the heat and let stand, covered, for 5 minutes. Transfer the vegetables to a strainer and press lightly.

2 Meanwhile, in a small bowl, blend the pesto with the goat cheese. On a lightly floured surface, roll out the puff pastry to a 13-inch square; trim the square to 12 inches. Prick the pastry all over with a fork and invert it onto the parchment-lined baking sheet.

3 Spread the goat cheese all over the pastry, leaving a 1-inch border all around. Top with the squash mixture. Arrange the tomato slices on the tart and sprinkle with salt and white pepper. Fold up the sides, pressing the corners together. Trim any excess pastry at the corners. Brush the pastry with the egg wash and bake in the lower third of the oven for about 45 minutes, until the edges are golden and the bottom is completely cooked through. Sprinkle with the olives, cut into squares and serve right away.

MAKE AHEAD The squash-and-tomato tart can be assembled and refrigerated for 2 hours before baking.

WINE *Bright, herbal Sauvignon Blanc: 2010 Veramonte Reserva.*

JERRY TRAUNFELD

Chard & Goat Cheese Strudel

WITH INDIAN FLAVORS

chef way

❯❯ *Jerry Traunfeld traveled through India in 2007, picking up inspiration for the small plates he now serves at his Seattle restaurant Poppy. He makes the dough for these innovative East-West strudels from scratch—pulling it paper-thin on a countertop—and seasons the strudels with* ajwain *seed, an Indian spice that tastes like caraway.*

easy way

❯❯ *Packaged frozen phyllo dough replaces homemade.*

❯❯ *Home cooks can use caraway seeds instead of the obscure* ajwain.

INGREDIENTS 6 servings

- 2 tablespoons extra-virgin olive oil
- 1 teaspoon fennel seeds
- ½ teaspoon cumin seeds
- ¼ teaspoon caraway seeds
- 1 small onion, finely chopped
- 2 garlic cloves, minced
- 1 bunch of Swiss chard (about 12 ounces), stems finely chopped and leaves coarsely chopped
- Salt and freshly ground pepper
- 4 ounces fresh goat cheese (½ cup)
- 4 sheets of phyllo dough, plus more in case of tearing
- 4 tablespoons unsalted butter, melted

ACTIVE 35 minutes   **TOTAL** 1 hour 30 minutes

1 In a large skillet, heat the oil until shimmering. Add the fennel, cumin and caraway seeds and cook over high heat until fragrant, about 30 seconds. Add the onion, garlic and chopped chard stems and cook over high heat, stirring occasionally, until softened, about 6 minutes. Add the chard leaves, season with salt and pepper and cook over high heat until the leaves are softened and any liquid has evaporated, about 8 minutes. Let cool, then fold in the goat cheese. Season with salt and pepper.

2 Preheat the oven to 375° and line a baking sheet with parchment paper. On a work surface, butter and stack the 4 sheets of phyllo dough; butter the top sheet. Spread the chard filling along a long edge, leaving about 1 inch of phyllo at each end. Roll up the phyllo to form a long cylinder, tucking in the ends as you go. Transfer the strudel to the baking sheet, seam side down, and brush with butter. Bake for about 35 minutes, until golden and crisp. Let cool for 20 minutes, then cut into 12 pieces and serve.

WINE *Tangy, citrusy Vermentino: 2009 Argiolas Costamolino.*

JOSE GARCES
Shrimp & Chorizo Flatbreads

chef way

❯❯ *For his stellar flatbreads, Jose Garces of Philadelphia's Amada prepares fresh coca dough, Spain's answer to pizza dough. He also cooks dried garbanzos for the bean puree he spreads on top.*

easy way

❯❯ *Store-bought pitas fill in for the traditional coca dough.*

❯❯ *The flatbreads are spread with good-quality prepared hummus.*

INGREDIENTS 8 servings

One 14-ounce can diced tomatoes, drained, ¼ cup of the juices reserved
2 tablespoons extra-virgin olive oil
1 tablespoon honey
1 tablespoon white wine vinegar
1 teaspoon chopped thyme
1 small shallot, minced
1 garlic clove, minced
2 tablespoons coarsely chopped flat-leaf parsley

Pinch of crushed red pepper
Salt and freshly ground black pepper
½ cup prepared hummus
4 pocketless pita breads
½ cup thinly sliced chorizo (2 ounces)
½ pound shelled and deveined medium shrimp, halved lengthwise
¼ pound Manchego cheese, shredded (1 cup)

TOTAL 30 minutes

1 Preheat the oven to 500° and position a rack in the center. In a medium bowl, mix the drained tomatoes and their reserved juices with the olive oil, honey, vinegar, thyme, shallot, garlic, parsley and crushed red pepper; season with salt and black pepper.

2 Spread the hummus on the pita breads and top with the chorizo, shrimp and Manchego. Bake directly on the oven rack for about 4 minutes, or until the shrimp are cooked and the cheese is melted. Transfer the shrimp-and-chorizo flatbreads to a work surface. Using a slotted spoon, top with the tomato dressing. Quarter the flatbreads and serve at once.

MAKE AHEAD The tomato dressing can be refrigerated overnight. Bring to room temperature before spooning onto the flatbreads.

WINE *Spicy, medium-bodied Tempranillo: 2007 Bodegas Montecillo Crianza.*

JERRY TRAUNFELD

Leek & Mushroom Croquettes

chef way

» *Dried porcini mushrooms flavor Jerry Traunfeld's crisp, creamy-centered croquettes, which he serves as walnut-size balls at his Seattle restaurant Poppy.*

easy way

» *Rather than dried porcini, this recipe uses fresh shiitake mushrooms, which don't need to be soaked.*

» *These larger croquettes take less time to form and fry.*

INGREDIENTS Makes 12 croquettes

5 tablespoons unsalted butter	1 cup milk
2 leeks, white and tender green parts only, thinly sliced	½ cup shredded Gruyère cheese
¼ pound shiitake mushrooms, stemmed and caps thinly sliced	¼ cup freshly grated Parmigiano-Reggiano cheese
Salt and freshly ground pepper	2 large eggs beaten with 2 tablespoons water
1 teaspoon chopped thyme	1½ cups *panko* (Japanese bread crumbs)
1 teaspoon chopped oregano	Vegetable oil, for frying
3 tablespoons all-purpose flour, plus more for coating	

ACTIVE 40 minutes **TOTAL** 3 hours

1 In a large skillet, melt 2 tablespoons of the butter. Add the leeks and shiitake, season with salt and pepper and cook over high heat, stirring frequently, until the leeks and mushrooms are softened and beginning to brown, about 7 minutes. Add the thyme and oregano to the vegetables and transfer to a medium bowl.

2 In a small saucepan, melt the remaining 3 tablespoons of butter. Whisk in the 3 tablespoons of flour and cook over high heat until bubbling, about 1 minute. Add the milk and cook, whisking constantly, until very thick and bubbling, about 3 minutes. Scrape the mixture into the bowl with the vegetables. Add the cheeses, season with salt and pepper and stir until evenly combined.

3 Lay an 18-inch-long piece of plastic wrap on a work surface. Spoon the croquette mixture onto the plastic in a 12-inch strip. Roll up the plastic, pressing the mixture into a 14-inch log, and twist the ends. Freeze the log until very firm, about 2 hours.

4 Fill 3 shallow bowls with flour, the beaten eggs and the *panko* and line a large baking sheet with wax paper. Unwrap the log and cut it into 12 pieces. Using floured hands, pat each piece into a 2-inch round patty, about ¾ inch thick. Dip each patty in the flour, then dip in the eggs and coat with *panko*, pressing to help it adhere. Set the croquettes on the baking sheet and freeze for 15 minutes.

5 In a large skillet, heat ½ inch of oil to 375°. Add the croquettes and fry over high heat, turning once or twice, until golden and crisp, about 5 minutes. Drain on paper towels and serve hot.

SERVE WITH A green salad.

MAKE AHEAD The croquettes can be prepared through Step 3 and refrigerated overnight.

WINE *Light-bodied, earthy Beaujolais: 2009 Clos de la Roilette Fleurie.*

JONATHON SAWYER

Curried Spaghetti Squash & Chickpea Toasts

chef way

❱❱ *Spaghetti squash, which separates into spaghetti-like strands when cooked, is the star of this vegetarian appetizer. At Cleveland's Greenhouse Tavern, Jonathon Sawyer combines the squash with his own curry spice blend and chickpeas that he's cooked himself, then spreads the mixture on toasts. He even uses the squash's seeds, roasting them for a garnish.*

easy way

❱❱ *Using store-bought curry paste and canned chickpeas reduces the prep time by hours.*

❱❱ *Toasted pumpkin seeds from the supermarket stand in for the homemade garnish.*

INGREDIENTS 6 servings

1 small spaghetti squash (about 3 pounds), halved and seeded
¼ cup plus 2 tablespoons extra-virgin olive oil
Salt and freshly ground black pepper
1 onion, chopped
1 carrot, finely chopped
1 tablespoon ground coriander
1½ teaspoons ground cumin
½ teaspoon crushed red pepper
½ teaspoon finely grated orange zest
1½ teaspoons Madras curry paste or curry powder
One 15-ounce can chickpeas, drained
½ cup water
½ cup chopped cilantro
Grilled peasant bread and toasted pumpkin seeds, for serving

ACTIVE 30 minutes **TOTAL** 1 hour

1 Preheat the oven to 350°. Place the halved spaghetti squash cut side up on a baking sheet and brush it with 2 tablespoons of the olive oil. Season with salt and black pepper. Roast the spaghetti squash for about 45 minutes, until the flesh is tender and lightly browned in spots. Let cool slightly.

2 Meanwhile, in a large skillet, heat the remaining ¼ cup of olive oil. Add the chopped onion and carrot and cook over moderate heat, stirring, until they are just softened, about 5 minutes. Add the coriander, cumin, crushed red pepper, grated orange zest and curry paste and cook, stirring, until fragrant, about 1 minute. Add the drained chickpeas and the water and simmer until the vegetables are very tender and the liquid has evaporated, about 5 minutes.

3 Using a fork, rake the squash into strands; you should have about 2½ cups of squash. Add the chopped cilantro and squash to the curry and season with salt. Serve the curried squash over grilled peasant bread, garnished with toasted pumpkin seeds.

MAKE AHEAD The curried squash can be refrigerated overnight. Let come to room temperature and add the cilantro just before serving.

WINE *Tropical fruit–scented Chenin Blanc: 2009 Raats Original.*

JOSE GARCES

Warm Piquillo & Crab Dip

chef way

❱❱ *To make this classic Spanish tapa at Amada in Philadelphia, Jose Garces stuffs crab salad into piquillo peppers before roasting them.*

easy way

❱❱ *Instead of stuffing individual piquillo peppers, it's much simpler to spread the crab mixture in a dish, top it with pepper slices, then broil until warm and melty.*

INGREDIENTS 4 servings

- 1 pound lump crabmeat, picked over for shell
- ¼ cup mayonnaise
- ¼ cup crème fraîche
- 2 tablespoons chopped flat-leaf parsley
- 2 tablespoons snipped chives
- 1 tablespoon Dijon mustard
- 2 teaspoons fresh lemon juice
- ¼ pound Manchego cheese, shredded (1 cup)
- One 9-ounce jar piquillo peppers, drained and cut into strips

TOTAL 25 minutes

Preheat the broiler. In a bowl, combine the crab, mayonnaise, crème fraîche, parsley, chives, mustard, lemon juice and ¾ cup of the Manchego. Spread in an 8-by-11-inch baking dish. Top with the piquillos and sprinkle with the remaining Manchego. Broil for 5 minutes, or until the cheese is melted and the dip is heated through. Serve right away.

SERVE WITH Crusty bread or crostini.

WINE *Zesty, slightly sparkling Spanish white: 2010 Xarmant Txakolina.*

JERRY TRAUNFELD

Roasted Cauliflower & Sesame Spread

chef way

» *During happy hour at Seattle's Poppy, guests can sample five* thalis *(Indian-influenced tapas-like snacks) for five dollars, including dishes like this bright, tangy spread. To make it, Jerry Traunfeld toasts and grinds whole coriander seeds before pureeing them with roasted cauliflower, tahini, lemon juice and cilantro.*

easy way

» *Whether in a mortar or a spice grinder, crushing spices takes time. This recipe calls for preground coriander instead.*

INGREDIENTS Makes 2 cups

1 head of cauliflower (2 pounds), halved crosswise and thinly sliced
¼ cup vegetable oil
1½ tablespoons minced fresh ginger
1½ teaspoons ground coriander

Kosher salt
3 tablespoons tahini (sesame paste)
3 tablespoons fresh lemon juice
3 tablespoons chopped cilantro
Sesame seeds
Pita bread or chips, for serving

ACTIVE 15 minutes **TOTAL** 1 hour

1 Preheat the oven to 450°. In a large bowl, toss the cauliflower with the oil, ginger and coriander and season with salt. Spread the cauliflower on a rimmed baking sheet and roast for about 40 minutes, stirring once or twice, until tender and lightly browned in spots. Let cool slightly.

2 Transfer the cauliflower to a food processor. Add the tahini and lemon juice and pulse to a chunky puree; season with salt. Add the cilantro and pulse just until incorporated. Transfer to a bowl and sprinkle with sesame seeds. Serve warm, with pita bread or chips.

SERVE WITH Olives.
MAKE AHEAD The cauliflower-sesame spread can be refrigerated overnight. Let come to room temperature before serving.

DANIEL BOULUD

Warm Camembert with Wild Mushroom Fricassee

chef way

» *Daniel Boulud of New York City's renowned Daniel makes this oozy appetizer with Vacherin Mont-d'Or, a creamy cow's milk cheese from Switzerland that's often served warm and eaten like fondue. It's available at top cheese shops.*

easy way

» *Camembert is as rich and runny as Vacherin Mont-d'Or but much easier to find (and less expensive, too).*

INGREDIENTS 4 servings

½ cup walnut pieces
One 8-ounce wheel of ripe Camembert in its wooden box, at room temperature
1 tablespoon walnut oil
¾ pound wild mushrooms, trimmed, caps thinly sliced

Salt and freshly ground pepper
1 shallot, minced
2 tablespoons chopped flat-leaf parsley
2 large sage leaves, minced
Sourdough toasts, for serving

TOTAL 30 minutes

1 Preheat the oven to 350°. Spread the walnut pieces on a baking sheet and toast in the oven for about 7 minutes, until lightly browned. Lower the oven temperature to 300°.

2 Remove the Camembert from the box and unwrap it. Put the cheese back in the bottom half of the box and set it on a baking sheet. Bake for about 10 minutes, until soft.

3 Meanwhile, in a large skillet, heat the walnut oil. Add the mushrooms and season with salt and pepper. Cover and cook over moderate heat, stirring occasionally, until softened, about 5 minutes. Uncover and cook, stirring, until lightly browned, 3 minutes longer. Add the shallot and cook until softened, 2 minutes. Stir in the parsley and sage; season with salt and pepper.

4 Invert the Camembert onto a platter. Stir the walnuts into the mushrooms and spoon over the cheese. Serve with the toasts.

WINE *Light, fruit-driven red: 2009 Georges Duboeuf Jean Descombes Morgon.*

ERIC AND SOPHIE BANH

Grilled Beef Rolls

chef way

» *At Monsoon in Seattle, Eric and Sophie Banh follow Vietnamese tradition and wrap their beef rolls in* la lot *leaves, which are similar to Japanese shiso. They buy the leaves fresh from Hawaii every week.*

easy way

» *Grape leaves are an excellent alternative to* la lot. *(They're sold in jars at Mediterranean and Greek specialty markets.)*

INGREDIENTS Makes 12 rolls

- ¼ cup plus 1 tablespoon vegetable oil, plus more for brushing
- 1 tablespoon Asian fish sauce
- 1 fresh lemongrass stalk, tender inner white bulb only, minced
- ½ teaspoon Chinese five-spice powder
- 1½ teaspoons honey
- 4 garlic cloves—1 minced, 3 very thinly sliced

Kosher salt

- ½ pound flank steak, thinly sliced across the grain into ¼-inch-thick slices, then halved crosswise
- 12 large grape leaves from a jar
- ½ small jicama, peeled and cut into 2-by-¼-inch matchsticks
- 24 small basil leaves
- 2 scallions, minced
- 2 tablespoons chopped unsalted roasted peanuts

TOTAL 1 hour

1 Light a grill or preheat a grill pan. In a medium bowl, mix 1 tablespoon of the oil with the fish sauce, lemongrass, five-spice powder, honey, minced garlic and ½ teaspoon of salt. Add the flank steak and toss to coat.

2 Using scissors, snip off the stems from the grape leaves and spread a few of the leaves out on a work surface. Place 2 slices of the garlic in the center of each leaf. Top with 2 slices of steak, 2 pieces of jicama and 2 basil leaves. Roll up the leaves into tight cylinders, tucking in the sides as you roll. Repeat with the remaining grape leaves, garlic, steak, jicama and basil. Thread the rolls onto 4 pairs of skewers, so that each pair holds 3 rolls. Lightly brush the skewered rolls with oil.

3 In a small skillet, heat the remaining ¼ cup of vegetable oil until just beginning to smoke. Remove the skillet from the heat and add the scallions and ½ teaspoon of salt. Immediately pour the hot scallion oil into a ramekin.

4 Grill the beef rolls over moderately high heat, turning once, until lightly charred outside and firm, about 8 minutes. Transfer the rolls to a platter and drizzle the scallion oil on top. Sprinkle with the chopped peanuts and serve.

WINE *Spicy Oregon Pinot Noir: 2008 Rex Hill Willamette Valley.*

JERRY TRAUNFELD

Spice Crispies

chef way

» *For his version of* chevda, *an Indian snack mix, Jerry Traunfeld of Seattle's Poppy tosses puffed rice cereal with coconut, raisins, nuts and a variety of spices and flavorings, including fresh curry leaves and* amchoor *(tart dried-mango powder).*

easy way

» *This sweet-salty bar mix comes together nicely without the* amchoor *and curry leaves—lemon juice and fresh bay leaves are fine substitutes.*

INGREDIENTS Makes about 4 cups

- 2 cups Rice Krispies or other puffed rice cereal (2 ounces)
- ¼ cup salted roasted cashews
- ¼ cup salted roasted peanuts
- ¼ cup wide coconut flakes
- ¼ cup raisins
- 3 tablespoons peanut oil
- 1 teaspoon yellow mustard seeds
- ½ teaspoon fennel seeds
- ½ teaspoon cumin seeds
- ¼ teaspoon crushed red pepper
- 4 large fresh bay leaves
- 3 tablespoons light corn syrup
- 1 teaspoon fresh lemon juice
- ½ teaspoon kosher salt

ACTIVE 15 minutes **TOTAL** 45 minutes

1 Preheat the oven to 325° and line a baking sheet with parchment paper. In a large bowl, toss the puffed rice with the cashews, peanuts, coconut flakes and raisins.

2 In a small saucepan, heat the oil until shimmering. Add the mustard seeds and cook over moderately high heat until they begin to pop, about 1 minute. Add the fennel and cumin seeds, crushed red pepper and bay leaves and toast, stirring, until fragrant, about 1 minute. Add the corn syrup, lemon juice and salt and bring to a boil. Drizzle the hot syrup over the cereal and nuts and toss with a spoon until evenly coated.

3 Spread the mixture on the baking sheet and bake, stirring once or twice, until the nuts are golden, about 20 minutes. Let cool; discard the bay leaves. Transfer to a bowl and serve.

MAKE AHEAD The Spice Crispies can be stored in an airtight container at room temperature for up to 4 days.

RATHA CHAUPOLY

Cambodian Chicken & Rice Soup

WITH SHRIMP

chef way

❱❱ *To make this spicy and soothing chicken-and-rice soup, Ratha Chaupoly of New York City's Num Pang Sandwich Shops prepares his own chicken stock and roasts a whole bird, which he then cuts into chunks and adds to the broth.*

easy way

❱❱ *Using prepared stock and preroasted chicken significantly cuts back on prep time.*

INGREDIENTS 4 servings

One 3-pound rotisserie chicken
1 tablespoon vegetable oil
2 tablespoons minced fresh ginger
2 garlic cloves, minced
4 cups chicken stock or low-sodium broth
1 cup water
3 tablespoons Asian fish sauce
1 teaspoon honey
1 cup cooked jasmine rice
8 shelled and deveined medium shrimp, halved lengthwise (about ¼ pound)
2 tablespoons fresh lime juice
¼ cup chopped cilantro
2 tablespoons chopped basil
1 Thai chile, thinly sliced
Lime wedges, for serving

TOTAL 40 minutes

1 Cut the rotisserie chicken into legs, thighs, breasts and wings. Cut each breast crosswise through the bones into 3 pieces. Remove the thigh bones and cut each thigh in half.

2 In a large saucepan, heat the vegetable oil. Add the ginger and garlic and cook over moderate heat until softened, about 3 minutes. Add the chicken stock, water, fish sauce, honey and cooked rice and bring to a boil. Add the chicken pieces and simmer for 5 minutes. Stir in the shrimp and cook just until opaque, about 1 minute. Stir in the lime juice, cilantro, basil and chile and serve the soup right away, passing lime wedges at the table.

WINE *Citrusy, off-dry Australian Riesling: 2010 Frogmore Creek FGR.*

PINO MAFFEO

Thai Chicken Stew

WITH POTATO-CHIVE DUMPLINGS

chef way

》 *Pino Maffeo, a Food & Wine Best New Chef 2006, serves this vibrant, spicy, warming stew with gai lan (Chinese broccoli). Sautéed garlic chives stud his potato dumplings.*

easy way

》 *Baby bok choy, an easy-to-find Chinese green, is swapped in for the gai lan; regular chives are a good replacement for the garlic chives.*

INGREDIENTS 4 servings

- ½ pound baking potatoes, peeled and cut into 1-inch chunks
- 2 tablespoons canola oil
- 1 pound skinless, boneless chicken thighs, cut into 1-inch pieces
- 1 large onion, finely chopped
- 1 large jalapeño—halved, seeded and thinly sliced
- ¼ cup Asian fish sauce
- 3 cups chicken stock or low-sodium broth
- 2 tablespoons all-purpose flour, plus more for rolling
- 1 large egg yolk
- 2 tablespoons minced chives
- Salt
- 1 pound baby bok choy, cut into 1-inch pieces
- 1 tablespoon cornstarch dissolved in 1 tablespoon water
- 2 tablespoons shredded basil leaves
- Lime wedges, for serving

TOTAL 1 hour

1 Put the potatoes in a medium saucepan and cover with hot water. Cook over high heat until tender, about 12 minutes.

2 Meanwhile, heat the oil in a large, heavy casserole. Add the chicken and cook over high heat until lightly browned, 4 minutes. Add the onion and jalapeño and cook, stirring, until the onion is softened, 4 minutes. Add 3 tablespoons of the fish sauce and the stock and bring to a boil. Cover and cook over moderate heat until the chicken is just cooked through, about 10 minutes.

3 Using a slotted spoon, transfer the potatoes to a ricer and press them into a bowl. (Alternatively, mash the potatoes.) Reserve the potato water. Add the 2 tablespoons of flour, egg yolk, chives and ½ teaspoon of salt to the potatoes and stir until a stiff dough forms. Turn the dough out onto a heavily floured board and divide it in half. Roll each piece of dough into a ½-inch-thick rope. Cut the ropes into 1-inch pieces.

4 Add the bok choy to the stew and cook until crisp-tender, about 5 minutes. Add the cornstarch mixture and cook, stirring, until thickened, 1 minute.

5 Return the potato water to a boil and add the potato-chive dumplings. Cook over high heat until they rise to the surface, then simmer for 2 minutes. Using a slotted spoon, transfer the dumplings to the chicken stew. Add the basil and the remaining 1 tablespoon of fish sauce and simmer the stew for 2 to 3 minutes. Serve right away, with lime wedges.

WINE *Lemon-appley Chardonnay: 2009 Lioco Sonoma County.*

DANIEL BOULUD

Chilled Spring Pea Soup

chef way

» *Daniel Boulud's deliciously light and clean-tasting soup—a mix of sweet peas, favas, pea shoots, snap peas and snow peas—shows up on the menu at New York City's Daniel each spring. It's a labor-intensive recipe because the favas need to be shelled twice: once from the pod and again from their casings.*

easy way

» *This soup gets terrific flavor from sugar snaps and frozen baby peas. The troublesome fresh favas are omitted, as are the snow peas and pea shoots.*

INGREDIENTS 6 servings

- 8 slices of bacon
- 1 tablespoon extra-virgin olive oil
- 2 celery ribs, thinly sliced
- 1 onion, thinly sliced
- 1 leek, white and tender green parts only, thinly sliced
- 5 cups chicken stock or low-sodium broth
- Two 4-inch rosemary sprigs
- Salt and freshly ground white pepper
- ½ pound sugar snap peas, thinly sliced
- Two 10-ounce boxes frozen baby peas
- ¼ cup flat-leaf parsley leaves
- 1 cup heavy cream
- 1 garlic clove, minced

TOTAL 1 hour

1 In a medium soup pot, cook the bacon over moderate heat until browned and crisp, about 6 minutes. Transfer the bacon to a plate. Pour off the fat in the pot.

2 In the same pot, heat the olive oil. Add the celery, onion and leek and cook over moderately low heat, stirring occasionally, until softened but not browned, about 7 minutes. Add the chicken stock, 4 slices of the cooked bacon, 1 rosemary sprig and a pinch each of salt and white pepper. Simmer until the vegetables are very tender, about 15 minutes. Discard the bacon and rosemary. Using a slotted spoon, transfer the vegetables to a blender.

3 Meanwhile, bring a medium saucepan of salted water to a boil. Add the sugar snaps; cook for 3 minutes. Add the frozen baby peas and the parsley and cook just until heated through, about 1 minute; drain. Add the sugar snaps, baby peas and parsley to the blender; puree until smooth, adding a few tablespoons of the broth to loosen the mixture. Transfer the soup and the remaining broth to a large bowl set in a larger bowl of ice water to cool.

4 In a small saucepan, bring the heavy cream, minced garlic and remaining rosemary sprig to a boil. Simmer over low heat until slightly reduced, about 5 minutes, then strain the garlic cream into a bowl and let cool.

5 Ladle the chilled pea soup into bowls and drizzle with the garlic cream. Crumble the remaining 4 slices of bacon into the bowls and serve.

MAKE AHEAD The pea soup and garlic cream can be refrigerated separately for up to 2 days.

WINE *Brisk Austrian Grüner Veltliner: 2009 Weingut Fred Loimer Lois.*

TRINA HAHNEMANN

Nordic Winter Vegetable Soup

chef way

» *Danish chef Trina Hahnemann calls the root vegetables in this simple vegetarian soup "the gold of Nordic soil" because they're high in nutrients and grow well in cold climates. In addition to celery root and parsnips, Hahnemann uses parsley root, sometimes called Hamburg parsley.*

easy way

» *Parsley root, which is common in Europe but not the US, is cut from the recipe. Celery root and parsnips are satisfying on their own.*

INGREDIENTS 8 servings

- 2 tablespoons extra-virgin olive oil
- 1 large onion, thinly sliced
- 2 leeks, white and tender green parts only, thinly sliced
- 2 garlic cloves, minced
- 1 cup pearled barley
- 8 cups low-sodium vegetable broth
- 4 cups water
- 10 thyme sprigs
- 2 bay leaves
- 1½ pounds celery root, peeled and cut into ½-inch cubes
- 1 pound parsnips, peeled and cut into ½-inch pieces

Salt and freshly ground pepper
- 1 pound baby spinach
- 1 teaspoon freshly grated nutmeg

ACTIVE 20 minutes   **TOTAL** 1 hour

1 In a large pot, heat the oil. Add the onion, leeks and garlic and cook over moderate heat, stirring occasionally, until tender, about 5 minutes. Stir in the barley. Add the vegetable broth, water, thyme sprigs and bay leaves and bring to a boil. Add the celery root and parsnips and season with salt and pepper. Simmer over moderately low heat until the barley and root vegetables are tender, about 40 minutes. Discard the thyme sprigs and bay leaves.

2 Stir in the spinach and nutmeg and simmer for 5 minutes. Season the soup with salt and pepper and serve in deep bowls.

SERVE WITH Hearty whole-grain rye bread.

WINE *Green apple–scented Chardonnay: 2009 Calera Central Coast.*

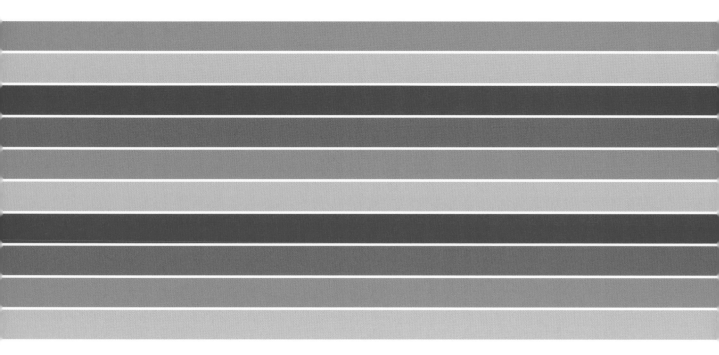

Salads

PINO MAFFEO

Green Salad

WITH GOAT CHEESE AND PISTACHIOS

chef way

》 *Pino Maffeo, a Food & Wine Best New Chef 2006, includes fennel, cucumber, bell pepper, carrots, bean sprouts and oven-dried tomatoes in his crisp salad. He uses red verjus (the unfermented juice of unripe grapes) to make a tangy vinaigrette.*

easy way

》 *The bean sprouts and oven-dried tomatoes are cut from the ingredient list.*

》 *Using a smaller amount of red wine vinegar, a pantry staple, approximates the gently acidic flavor of verjus.*

INGREDIENTS 4 servings

½ small shallot, minced
2 tablespoons red wine vinegar
¼ cup extra-virgin olive oil
Salt and freshly ground pepper
5 ounces mesclun greens
½ small fennel bulb, cored and thinly sliced
½ seedless cucumber, peeled and thinly sliced

½ red bell pepper, cored and thinly sliced
¼ small red onion, thinly sliced
1 avocado—peeled, pitted and thinly sliced
2 ounces crumbled fresh goat cheese
¼ cup roasted shelled pistachios

TOTAL 25 minutes

In a large bowl, whisk the chopped shallot with the red wine vinegar and olive oil. Season with salt and pepper. Add the mesclun greens, fennel, cucumber, bell pepper and onion and toss. Add the avocado slices and crumbled goat cheese, season with salt and pepper and gently toss the salad again. Sprinkle the pistachios on the salad and serve right away.

WINE *Fresh, minerally Italian white: 2009 Inama Vin Soave Classico.*

LIDIA BASTIANICH

Arugula Salad

WITH RICOTTA SALATA

chef way

» *When she serves this crunchy, nutty salad at New York City's Felidia, Lidia Bastianich likes to use young, tender dandelion greens, which she used to forage for as a child in Italy.*

easy way

» *Arugula stands in for the elusive young dandelion greens. Both are pleasantly bitter.*

INGREDIENTS 4 servings

¼ cup plus 2 tablespoons extra-virgin olive oil
2 tablespoons red wine vinegar
1 teaspoon honey
½ cup salted roasted almonds, coarsely chopped

3 bunches of arugula, thick stems discarded
Salt and freshly ground pepper
½ pound *ricotta salata* cheese, shaved with a peeler

TOTAL 30 minutes

In a blender or food processor, blend the olive oil, vinegar, honey and 2 tablespoons of the almonds until the almonds are finely chopped; transfer to a large bowl. Add the arugula, season with salt and pepper and toss. Top with the *ricotta salata,* sprinkle on the remaining almonds and serve the salad right away.

DONALD LINK

Iceberg Salad

WITH BLUE CHEESE DRESSING

chef way

» *Donald Link of Cochon in New Orleans makes his own mayonnaise for his easy-to-eat interpretation of the classic iceberg wedge salad. (He tears the lettuce to make a lovely base for the blue cheese dressing, bacon, onion and croutons.)*

easy way

» *Prepared mayo substitutes for homemade in the salad's delightfully creamy dressing.*

INGREDIENTS 6 servings

- 3 cups 1-inch-cubed crusty white bread
- ½ cup plus 1 tablespoon vegetable oil
- ¾ pound sliced bacon
- 1 garlic clove, crushed

Salt

- 2 tablespoons mayonnaise
- 3 tablespoons buttermilk
- 1½ tablespoons red wine vinegar
- 1 teaspoon Dijon mustard

Cayenne pepper

- ¼ pound blue cheese, preferably Maytag, crumbled (¾ cup)
- 1 head of iceberg lettuce, cut into 1-inch pieces
- ½ small red onion, thinly sliced
- 1 celery rib, thinly sliced

TOTAL 30 minutes

1 Preheat the oven to 350°. On a baking sheet, toss the bread cubes with 1 tablespoon of the vegetable oil and toast for 15 minutes, stirring once or twice, until the bread is golden and crisp.

2 Meanwhile, in a large skillet, cook the bacon over moderately high heat, turning once, until crisp, about 6 minutes. Drain the bacon on paper towels and crumble.

3 In a small bowl, using the back of a spoon, mash the garlic to a paste with a pinch of salt. Whisk in the mayonnaise, buttermilk, red wine vinegar and mustard. Gradually whisk in the remaining ½ cup of vegetable oil and season the dressing with salt and cayenne pepper. Stir in the blue cheese.

4 In a large bowl, toss the lettuce, onion, celery, bacon and croutons with the dressing and serve right away.

MAKE AHEAD The bacon and dressing can be refrigerated separately overnight. The croutons can be stored overnight in an airtight container at room temperature.

JOSE GARCES
Spinach Salad
WITH WARM BACON VINAIGRETTE

chef way

» *Preparing the salad dressing as Jose Garces does at Philadelphia's Amada is a two-step process: First he marinates chopped shallots in vinegar, mustard and thyme, then he adds the mixture to warm bacon fat in a skillet.*

easy way

» *The bacon vinaigrette is made start-to-finish in a skillet (no marinating involved), then tossed with the sliced plums and baby spinach in a bowl.*

INGREDIENTS 4 servings

3 strips of thickly sliced lean bacon, cut into ¼-inch strips
2 tablespoons extra-virgin olive oil
1 shallot, minced
2 tablespoons sherry vinegar
1 tablespoon whole-grain mustard
1 teaspoon chopped thyme
2 small plums, sliced into thin wedges, or 4 fresh purple figs, quartered

5 ounces baby spinach
Salt and freshly ground pepper
¼ cup marcona or other salted roasted almonds, coarsely chopped
2 ounces crumbled blue cheese, such as Cabrales
¼ pound thinly sliced serrano ham or prosciutto (8 slices)

TOTAL 25 minutes

1 In a large skillet, cook the bacon in the olive oil over moderately high heat until browned and crisp, about 6 minutes. Remove from the heat and stir in the shallot, vinegar, mustard and thyme.

2 Scrape the dressing into a large bowl. Add the plums and spinach, season with salt and pepper and toss. Add the nuts and crumbled blue cheese and toss again. Transfer the salad to plates, top with the sliced ham and serve.

WINE *Fruit-forward California rosé: 2010 Edmunds St. John Bone-Jolly Gamay Noir Rosé.*

RATHA CHAUPOLY

Asian Pea Salad

WITH HONEYED BACON

chef way

❭❭ *Ratha Chaupoly of New York City's Num Pang Sandwich Shops typically includes crispy slices of Chinese sausage in this salad. He makes the spicy oil for the vinaigrette himself.*

easy way

❭❭ *Instead of Chinese sausage, which isn't readily available, thick slices of bacon are brushed with a honey-soy mix, then broiled until crisp.*

❭❭ *Store-bought chile oil, either plain or sesame-flavored (available at Asian food markets), is a good alternative to homemade.*

INGREDIENTS 4 servings

- 6 thick slices of maple-cured bacon (about 6 ounces)
- 2 tablespoons honey
- 1 tablespoon soy sauce
- ½ teaspoon Chinese five-spice powder
- 3 tablespoons pure olive oil
- 2 tablespoons fresh lime juice
- ½ teaspoon finely grated lime zest
- 1 tablespoon Asian fish sauce
- 1 tablespoon chile oil
- Salt and freshly ground pepper
- ½ pound snow peas, julienned
- 6 ounces snow pea shoots (8 cups)
- 2 tablespoons torn basil leaves
- 2 tablespoons torn mint leaves

TOTAL 30 minutes

1 Preheat the broiler and position a rack 8 inches from the heat. Arrange the bacon slices on a baking sheet in a single layer. In a small bowl, stir together the honey, soy sauce and five-spice powder and brush liberally over the bacon. Broil for 10 minutes, turning once, until the bacon slices are browned and crisp. Transfer the bacon to a work surface and cut into ½-inch pieces. Let the bacon cool.

2 In a large bowl, whisk the olive oil with the lime juice, lime zest, fish sauce and chile oil and season with salt and pepper. Add the snow peas, pea shoots, basil, mint and bacon and toss. Serve right away.

WINE *Vibrant Albariño: 2009 Do Ferreiro Rias Baixas.*

MICHAEL WHITE

Crunchy Vegetable Salad

WITH RICOTTA CROSTINI

chef way

» *Michael White makes his fennel-and-asparagus salad at Marea in New York City with a variety of herbs, such as chervil and lemon balm.*

easy way

» *The salad is equally delicious made with just two familiar herbs, basil and tarragon.*

INGREDIENTS 6 servings

- 6 slices of rustic white bread
- ¼ cup extra-virgin olive oil, plus more for brushing and drizzling
- 1 garlic clove, halved
- ¾ cup fresh ricotta cheese
- Salt and freshly ground black pepper
- 2 tablespoons white balsamic vinegar
- 1 tablespoon Dijon mustard
- 6 large radishes, thinly sliced
- 1 fennel bulb, cored and thinly sliced
- ½ pound asparagus, thinly sliced on the bias
- 1 large carrot, finely julienned
- ½ small seedless cucumber, peeled and cut into ½-inch chunks
- 1 head of Boston lettuce, torn into bite-size pieces
- 2 tablespoons shredded basil leaves
- 1 tablespoon coarsely chopped tarragon

TOTAL 30 minutes

1 Preheat the broiler. Brush the bread on both sides with olive oil and place on a baking sheet. Broil 4 inches from the heat for about 1 minute per side, until golden. Lightly rub the toasts with the cut sides of the garlic and spread with the ricotta. Season with salt and pepper and drizzle with olive oil.

2 In a large bowl, whisk the vinegar with the mustard and the ¼ cup of olive oil; season with salt and pepper. Add the radishes, fennel, asparagus, carrot, cucumber, lettuce, basil and tarragon; toss gently to coat. Serve the salad right away, with the ricotta crostini.

WINE *Crisp, minerally Italian white: 2009 Fontezoppa Verdicchio di Matelica.*

RYAN HARDY

Kale & Apple Salad

WITH PANCETTA AND CANDIED PECANS

chef way

❯❯ *Kale is a marvelous green for salads because it's hearty enough to handle hefty ingredients like nuts and meat, plus it doesn't wilt as it sits on the table. When Ryan Hardy made this salad at Montagna at the Little Nell hotel in Aspen, Colorado, he deep-fried the pecans.*

easy way

❯❯ *Toasting the pecans in the oven is quicker (and less messy) than deep-frying.*

INGREDIENTS 12 servings

2 cups pecans
½ cup confectioners' sugar
½ teaspoon cayenne pepper
Kosher salt
¼ cup extra-virgin olive oil
6 ounces thickly sliced pancetta, finely diced
¼ cup white wine vinegar
2 tablespoons caper brine (from a jar of capers)
3 tablespoons pure maple syrup

Freshly ground black pepper
2 Granny Smith apples, cut into matchsticks
1 large head of radicchio, shredded
One 8-ounce bunch of kale— stems discarded, leaves finely shredded
3 tablespoons snipped chives
1 tablespoon chopped tarragon
2 ounces shaved pecorino

TOTAL 45 minutes

1 Preheat the oven to 350°. In a bowl, cover the pecans with water. Transfer to a sieve and shake out the water. In another bowl, whisk the confectioners' sugar, cayenne and 1½ teaspoons of salt. Add the pecans and toss. Transfer to a sieve and shake off the excess coating. Arrange the pecans on a parchment paper–lined baking sheet and bake for 10 to 12 minutes, until the sugar is lightly caramelized and the pecans are golden.

2 In a skillet, heat the oil with the pancetta and cook over moderate heat, stirring frequently, until the pancetta is browned, 6 minutes. Strain the pan drippings into a large bowl; whisk in the vinegar, caper brine and maple syrup and season the dressing with salt and black pepper. Add the apples, radicchio, kale, chives, tarragon and pecorino and toss. Mound the salad on plates, garnish with the pecans and pancetta and serve.

WINE *Substantial Rhône white blend: 2009 Tablas Creek Esprit de Beaucastel Blanc.*

GEORGE MENDES

Beet & Apple Salad

chef way

❯❯ *The menu changes regularly at New York City's Aldea. For this fall salad, George Mendes uses fresh horseradish and Gegenbauer cider vinegar, a rare Austrian import.*

easy way

❯❯ *Jarred horseradish takes the place of fresh.*

❯❯ *Supermarket apple-cider vinegar has the same tangy, acidic flavor as imported.*

INGREDIENTS 8 servings

- 4 large beets (2½ pounds)
- 5 thyme sprigs
- ½ cup extra-virgin olive oil, plus more for drizzling
- Salt and freshly ground pepper
- ¼ cup apple-cider vinegar
- 1 teaspoon Dijon mustard
- 3 tablespoons prepared horseradish
- ⅓ cup salted pistachios, chopped
- 1 green apple, thinly sliced

ACTIVE 30 minutes **TOTAL** 2 hours 15 minutes

1 Preheat the oven to 375°. In a baking dish, lightly drizzle the beets and thyme with olive oil. Season with salt and pepper. Cover with foil and roast until the beets are tender, about 1 hour and 45 minutes. Let cool, then peel the beets and cut them into ¾-inch dice.

2 In a large bowl, whisk the vinegar with the mustard. Whisk in the ½ cup of olive oil until emulsified. Add the horseradish and season with salt and pepper; toss with the beets and pistachios. Transfer the beets to a platter, top with the apple and serve.

MOURAD LAHLOU

Beet & Pickled Cherry Salad

WITH CRISPY SHALLOTS

chef way

» *Moroccans often start a big meal with several small plates, including one with marinated beets. At Aziza in San Francisco, Mourad Lahlou combines roasted beets with a few well-placed mizuna leaves to create a delicate, pretty salad.*

easy way

» *No need to be so precise or precious with the plating. This home version is more rustic and hearty.*

INGREDIENTS 4 servings

- 2 large beets, quartered
- ¼ cup extra-virgin olive oil
- 4 thyme sprigs
- 3 garlic cloves, smashed
- ½ cup red wine vinegar
- Salt and freshly ground black pepper
- ½ cup dried sour cherries (3 ounces)
- 1 teaspoon fennel seeds
- ¼ cup sugar
- Canola oil, for frying
- 4 large shallots, very thinly sliced
- 1 tablespoon fresh lemon juice
- 4 ounces mizuna or mesclun

ACTIVE 45 minutes **TOTAL** 2 hours 30 minutes

1 Preheat the oven to 350°. In a small baking dish, toss the beets with the olive oil, thyme, garlic and ¼ cup of the vinegar and season with salt and black pepper. Cover tightly with foil and roast for about 1½ hours, until fork-tender. Let cool slightly.

2 Meanwhile, in a small saucepan, combine the dried cherries with the fennel seeds, sugar, ¾ cup of water and the remaining ¼ cup of vinegar and bring to a simmer. Remove from the heat and let the cherries stand for 30 minutes.

3 In a large saucepan, heat 2 inches of canola oil over moderately high heat until shimmering. Add the shallots; cook over moderate heat, stirring, until golden brown, about 10 minutes. Using a slotted spoon, transfer the shallots to paper towels to drain.

4 Peel the beets and slice them ¼ inch thick. Strain the beet cooking liquid into a large bowl. Spoon 2 tablespoons of the cherry pickling liquid into the bowl along with the lemon juice and whisk to combine. Season the dressing with salt and black pepper. Strain the cherries and discard the remaining pickling liquid.

5 Arrange the beets on a platter. Toss the mizuna and cherries in the bowl with the dressing. Mound the greens over the beets, garnish with the fried shallots and serve.

WINE *Robust, juicy rosé: 2010 Tapeña.*

SHAWN MCCLAIN
Crab Salad
WITH CAESAR VINAIGRETTE

chef way

» *Shawn McClain of Chicago's Green Zebra uses a mortar and pestle to pound the ingredients for this piquant anchovy-and-Parmesan dressing, which he tosses with lettuce, crabmeat and home-roasted pimiento peppers.*

easy way

» *A blender does the work of the mortar and pestle.*

» *Home cooks can buy jarred peppers instead of roasting them.*

INGREDIENTS 4 servings

- 8 white anchovies (see Note)
- 1 garlic clove
- 2 tablespoons red wine vinegar
- 1 teaspoon Dijon mustard
- 1 teaspoon Worcestershire sauce
- ¼ cup extra-virgin olive oil
- Salt and freshly ground pepper
- ¼ cup freshly grated Parmigiano-Reggiano cheese
- 1 pound jumbo lump crabmeat, picked over for shell
- 1 tablespoon snipped chives
- 1½ teaspoons chopped tarragon
- ¼ cup finely diced roasted red pepper
- ½ pound baby romaine lettuce leaves

TOTAL 30 minutes

1 In a blender or mini processor, combine 4 of the anchovies with the garlic, vinegar, mustard and Worcestershire sauce and puree until smooth. With the machine on, add the olive oil and blend until incorporated. Season the vinaigrette with salt and pepper; add the Parmesan and blend briefly.

2 In a large bowl, gently toss the crab, chives, tarragon and red pepper with the vinaigrette. Add the romaine and toss. Transfer to plates, top with the remaining 4 anchovies and serve.

NOTE Marinated white anchovies are available at Italian markets, specialty food stores and in the deli case at some supermarkets.

WINE *Berry-rich, juicy rosé: 2010 Francis Coppola Sofia.*

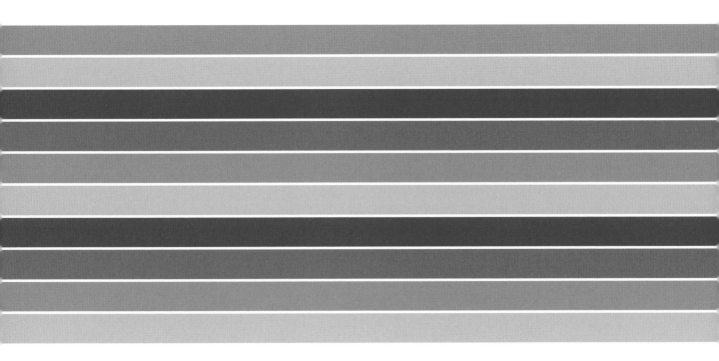

Pasta

MARIO BATALI

Bucatini

ALL'AMATRICIANA

chef way

» *This classic dish originated in a hill town outside Rome called Amatrice. At Babbo in New York City, Mario Batali serves a prime version of it, tossing the long, hollow pasta strands with house-cured* guanciale *(pork jowl) and a spicy house-made tomato sauce.*

easy way

» *Home cooks can replace the* guanciale *with pancetta, which is easier to find.*

» *A good jarred tomato sauce stands in for homemade.*

INGREDIENTS 4 servings

½ pound thinly sliced pancetta, coarsely chopped
1 red onion, thinly sliced
3 garlic cloves, thinly sliced
1½ teaspoons crushed red pepper
12 ounces prepared tomato sauce

Kosher salt
1 pound bucatini
½ cup flat-leaf parsley leaves
Grated Pecorino Romano cheese, for serving

TOTAL 30 minutes

1 In a large, deep skillet, cook the pancetta over moderate heat, stirring frequently, until lightly browned, about 6 minutes. Using a slotted spoon, transfer the pancetta to a plate. Pour off all but 2 tablespoons of the fat in the skillet. Add the onion, garlic and crushed red pepper and cook over moderately high heat, stirring occasionally, until the onion is lightly browned, about 6 minutes. Return the pancetta to the skillet. Add the tomato sauce, season with salt and simmer until very thick, about 10 minutes.

2 Meanwhile, in a pot of boiling salted water, cook the pasta until al dente. Drain the pasta, reserving ½ cup of the cooking water.

3 Add the pasta to the sauce along with the parsley and the reserved cooking water and stir over moderately high heat until the pasta is evenly coated, 2 minutes. Serve the pasta in bowls, passing the cheese at the table.

WINE *Medium-bodied Barbera d'Alba: 2007 Cantina Terre del Barolo.*

DANIEL BOULUD

Orecchiette Bolognese
WITH CHESTNUTS

chef way

❯❯ *Daniel Boulud of New York City's celebrated restaurant Daniel tops house-made orecchiette (ear-shaped pasta) with a Bolognese sauce that includes venison, pork butt, chicken liver and veal stock. For a luxurious presentation, he tops the dish with fresh porcini mushrooms, chestnuts and butternut squash.*

easy way

❯❯ *The Bolognese sauce includes just ham and ground chuck.*

❯❯ *Store-bought dried orecchiette fills in for homemade pasta.*

❯❯ *The porcini and squash are omitted—the chestnuts alone add an elegant and unexpected touch.*

INGREDIENTS 6 servings

- 1¼ pounds thickly sliced smoked ham, torn into small pieces
- 2 tablespoons extra-virgin olive oil
- 1¼ pounds ground beef chuck
- Pinch of ground cloves
- 1 celery rib, finely chopped
- 1 carrot, finely chopped
- 1 onion, finely chopped
- 2 garlic cloves, minced
- 1 tablespoon finely chopped sage
- 1 tablespoon finely chopped rosemary
- ¼ teaspoon crushed red pepper
- 1½ cups dry red wine
- One 28-ounce can tomato puree
- 2 cups chicken stock or low-sodium broth
- Pinch of sugar
- Freshly ground black pepper
- 1 pound orecchiette
- ½ cup heavy cream
- 1 cup vacuum-packed chestnuts, coarsely chopped (4 ounces)
- 2 tablespoons very finely chopped flat-leaf parsley
- Salt
- Freshly grated Parmesan cheese, for serving

ACTIVE 40 minutes **TOTAL** 1 hour 30 minutes

1 Pulse the ham pieces in a food processor until coarsely chopped. In a large, deep casserole or Dutch oven, heat the oil. Add the chopped ham, beef chuck and cloves; cook over high heat, stirring once or twice, until the meat begins to brown, about 10 minutes.

2 Add the celery, carrot, onion and garlic to the casserole and cook, stirring, until the vegetables are barely softened, about 3 minutes. Stir in the sage, rosemary and crushed red pepper and cook until fragrant, 2 to 3 minutes. Add the red wine and cook until it is nearly evaporated, about 10 minutes. Add the tomato puree, chicken stock and sugar, season with black pepper and bring to a boil over moderately high heat. Simmer uncovered over low heat, stirring occasionally, until the Bolognese sauce is thick and reduced by half, about 45 minutes.

3 Meanwhile, in a large pot of boiling salted water, cook the orecchiette until al dente.

4 Stir the heavy cream into the Bolognese sauce and simmer for 5 minutes. Stir in the chopped chestnuts and parsley and season lightly with salt. Drain the pasta and transfer to a large bowl. Spoon the Bolognese sauce over the pasta and serve, passing the Parmesan at the table.

WINE *Spicy, cherry-rich Chianti Classico: 2007 Fèlsina Berardenga.*

CHRIS COSENTINO

Spaghetti with Anchovy Carbonara

chef way

» *To add briny, minerally flavor to his pasta, Chris Cosentino of San Francisco's Incanto shaves cured tuna heart over the dish right before serving. An egg yolk on top— which diners mix into the spaghetti themselves—forms a silky sauce.*

easy way

» *This recipe calls for anchovies rather than tuna heart.*

» *The egg yolks are tossed with all the other ingredients in the skillet.*

INGREDIENTS 4 servings

12 ounces spaghetti
¼ cup extra-virgin olive oil
3 large garlic cloves, thinly sliced
One 2-ounce can flat anchovies, drained and chopped
Pinch of Aleppo pepper or crushed red pepper
½ teaspoon finely grated lemon zest
1 tablespoon chopped oregano
¼ cup chopped flat-leaf parsley
2 large egg yolks
Salt and freshly ground black pepper

TOTAL 30 minutes

1 In a large pot of boiling salted water, cook the spaghetti until al dente. Drain the pasta, reserving ½ cup of the cooking water.

2 In a large, deep skillet, heat the olive oil with the garlic and anchovies and cook over moderately high heat until the anchovies have dissolved, about 2 minutes. Add the red pepper, lemon zest, oregano and parsley, then add the pasta and toss to coat. Remove the skillet from the heat.

3 In a small bowl, whisk the egg yolks with the reserved cooking water and add to the pasta. Cook over low heat, tossing, until the pasta is coated in a creamy sauce, about 1 minute. Season with salt and black pepper and serve.

WINE *Citrusy, minerally Italian white: 2009 Bisson Marea Vermentino.*

ANDREW CARMELLINI

Pappardelle with Lamb Ragù

chef way

» *At Locanda Verde in New York City, Andrew Carmellini serves fresh pappardelle with a ragù of house-ground lamb shoulder cooked in lamb stock. He tops the dish with fresh ricotta cheese and mint.*

easy way

» *Using store-bought pappardelle, ground lamb from a butcher and premade chicken stock shaves hours off the cooking time.*

INGREDIENTS 6 servings

- 3 tablespoons extra-virgin olive oil
- 1 carrot, finely diced
- 1 onion, finely diced
- 1 celery rib, finely diced
- 1½ pounds ground lamb
- 2 teaspoons ground coriander
- 1 teaspoon ground fennel seeds
- ½ teaspoon ground cumin
- 1 teaspoon chopped rosemary
- 1 teaspoon chopped thyme
- Salt and freshly ground pepper
- 1 tablespoon tomato paste
- ½ cup dry red wine
- One 28-ounce can diced tomatoes
- 1¼ cups chicken stock or low-sodium broth
- 12 ounces pappardelle
- 1 tablespoon unsalted butter
- ¾ cup fresh ricotta cheese
- 2 tablespoons chopped mint

ACTIVE 30 minutes   **TOTAL** 1 hour

1 In a large cast-iron casserole, heat 2 tablespoons of the oil. Add the carrot, onion and celery and cook over high heat, stirring occasionally, until slightly softened, 5 minutes. Add the lamb, coriander, fennel, cumin, rosemary and thyme; season with salt and pepper. Cook, stirring, until the liquid evaporates, 5 minutes. Stir in the tomato paste. Add the wine and cook until evaporated, 5 minutes. Add the tomatoes and their juices along with the stock and bring to a boil. Cover partially and cook over moderately low heat until the liquid is slightly reduced, 25 to 30 minutes.

2 Meanwhile, in a large pot of boiling salted water, cook the pasta until al dente. Drain, shaking well. Add the pasta to the sauce. Add the butter and the remaining 1 tablespoon of oil and toss over low heat. Serve the pasta in bowls, topped with the ricotta and mint.

WINE *Medium-bodied, berry-rich Barbera d'Alba: 2008 Vietti Tre Vigne.*

COREY LEE

Fettuccine with Chicken-Liver Sauce

chef way

» *Corey Lee makes fresh pasta to serve with his creamy chicken-liver sauce at Benu in San Francisco. Before sautéing the livers, he soaks them in milk for 12 hours to mellow their flavor.*

easy way

» *No need to make the fettuccine from scratch; it's quite easy to find high-quality fresh pasta in specialty stores.*

» *Soaking the livers for just one hour removes any metallic or harsh flavors and results in a rich sauce.*

INGREDIENTS 4 to 6 servings

½ pound chicken livers, trimmed
1 cup milk
1 tablespoon canola oil
1 large shallot, minced
1 garlic clove, minced
1 teaspoon chopped thyme
¼ cup dry sherry

4 tablespoons unsalted butter, cubed
Salt and freshly ground pepper
1 pound fresh fettuccine or tagliatelle
2 tablespoons snipped chives
2 cups quartered grape tomatoes

ACTIVE 30 minutes **TOTAL** 1 hour 30 minutes

1 In a medium bowl, cover the chicken livers with the milk and let stand for 1 hour. Drain and pat completely dry.

2 In a large skillet, heat the oil until shimmering. Add the chicken livers and cook over high heat until lightly browned on the bottoms, about 2 minutes. Turn the livers. Add the shallot, garlic and thyme to the skillet and cook until the shallot and garlic are fragrant and softened, about 2 minutes. Add the sherry and cook, scraping up any bits stuck to the bottom of the pan, until the liquid is evaporated and the livers are cooked through, about 2 minutes. Scrape the mixture into a food processor and pulse until chopped. With the machine on, add the butter and puree until smooth. Scrape the chicken-liver butter into a bowl and season with salt and pepper.

3 In a large pot of generously salted boiling water, cook the pasta until just al dente. Drain the pasta, reserving ¾ cup of the cooking water. Return the pasta to the pot. Add the chicken-liver butter, chives, tomatoes and the reserved pasta cooking water. Bring to a simmer over moderately low heat, tossing until the pasta is coated with the creamy sauce. Transfer to bowls and serve right away.

MAKE AHEAD The chicken-liver butter can be refrigerated overnight. Bring to room temperature before using.

WINE *Bright, cherry-rich Pinot Noir: 2008 Heron Sonoma County.*

MICHAEL WHITE

Angel Hair Pasta with Seafood & Zucchini

chef way

》 *Michael White of New York City's Marea is known for his spectacular fresh-pasta dishes. He serves this one with tender zucchini blossoms and seasoned house-made bread crumbs.*

easy way

》 *Dried pasta and packaged bread crumbs from the supermarket take the place of homemade.*

》 *Zucchini blossoms, which are very seasonal and somewhat difficult to find, are dropped in favor of julienned zucchini.*

INGREDIENTS 6 servings

- 6 tablespoons extra-virgin olive oil, plus more for drizzling
- 3 garlic cloves— 1 minced, 2 thinly sliced
- ½ teaspoon dried oregano
- ¾ cup *panko* (Japanese bread crumbs)

Kosher salt

- ½ teaspoon crushed red pepper
- 2 pounds mussels, scrubbed
- 1 cup dry white wine
- ½ pound baby squid, bodies cut into thin rings
- 1 pound angel hair pasta
- 1 pound small zucchini, julienned

TOTAL 45 minutes

1 In a large, deep skillet, combine 2 tablespoons of the olive oil with the minced garlic, oregano and *panko* and cook over moderate heat, stirring constantly, until the crumbs are golden and fragrant, about 7 minutes. Season the crumbs with salt and scrape them onto a plate; wipe out the skillet.

2 In the same skillet, heat the remaining ¼ cup of olive oil with the sliced garlic and crushed red pepper until fragrant, about 30 seconds. Add the mussels and white wine. Cover and cook until the shells have opened, about 5 minutes; discard any mussels that don't open. Add the squid to the skillet and cook just until firm, 1 minute. Using a slotted spoon, transfer the seafood to a large bowl.

3 Meanwhile, in a large pot of boiling salted water, cook the pasta until barely al dente. Drain; reserve ½ cup of the cooking water.

4 Add the pasta to the skillet along with the cooking water and the zucchini. Add the seafood and any accumulated juices and toss over moderate heat until the zucchini is cooked, about 1 minute. Transfer the pasta and seafood to bowls. Drizzle with olive oil and sprinkle with the seasoned crumbs. Serve right away.

WINE *Lively, floral northern Italian white: 2009 Livio Felluga Friulano.*

LIDIA BASTIANICH
Spinach & Ricotta Pappardelle

chef way

» *In her version of this dish at Felidia in New York City, Lidia Bastianich stuffs homemade ravioli with ricotta, leeks, scallions and spinach, then serves them in a butter-sage sauce.*

easy way

» *This quick recipe deconstructs Bastianich's ravioli: Wide, flat pappardelle noodles are simply stirred in a skillet with all the filling ingredients (except the labor-intensive leeks).*

INGREDIENTS 4 servings

- 12 ounces pappardelle
- 2 tablespoons extra-virgin olive oil
- 4 scallions, thinly sliced
- 1 tablespoon chopped sage
- 10 ounces baby spinach
- 2 tablespoons unsalted butter, cut into cubes
- 1 cup fresh ricotta cheese
- ¼ cup freshly grated Parmigiano-Reggiano cheese, plus more for serving

Salt and freshly ground pepper

TOTAL 30 minutes

1 In a large pot of boiling salted water, cook the pappardelle until al dente. Drain thoroughly, reserving 1 cup of the pasta cooking water.

2 Meanwhile, in a large, deep skillet, heat the olive oil. Add the scallions and sage and cook over high heat until lightly browned, 2 to 3 minutes. Add the spinach in large handfuls and cook, stirring, until wilted. Add the pasta, butter and ricotta and toss. Add ¾ cup of the reserved pasta cooking water and the ¼ cup of Parmigiano and season generously with salt and pepper. Cook over moderately low heat, tossing, until the sauce is thick and creamy, adding more of the pasta water as needed. Transfer the pappardelle to bowls and serve right away, with grated Parmigiano.

WINE *Fragrant, peach-inflected Soave Classico: 2009 Pieropan.*

ANDREW CARMELLINI

Gnocchi with Wild Mushrooms

chef way

❯❯ *After cooking homemade gnocchi in his own intense mushroom stock at New York City's Locanda Verde, Andrew Carmellini tosses them with porcini butter (blended with garlic, herbs and Parmesan) and white truffle shavings.*

easy way

❯❯ *Store-bought gnocchi and chicken stock substitute for homemade.*

❯❯ *The topping: Parmesan cheese and truffle oil (available at Whole Foods and specialty food stores).*

INGREDIENTS 6 servings

- 2 tablespoons extra-virgin olive oil
- 2 tablespoons unsalted butter
- 2 pounds mixed wild mushrooms, stemmed if necessary and thickly sliced (10 cups)
- 2 shallots, minced
- ¼ cup dry vermouth
- ¾ cup chicken stock or low-sodium broth
- ½ cup heavy cream
- 1 teaspoon chopped thyme

Salt and freshly ground pepper
- 2 pounds fresh or frozen prepared gnocchi
- ¼ cup plus 2 tablespoons freshly grated Parmesan cheese
- 1 teaspoon white truffle oil (optional)

TOTAL 30 minutes

1 Preheat the broiler. In a large ovenproof skillet, heat the olive oil with the butter. Add the mushrooms and shallots and cook over high heat, stirring occasionally, until browned, 12 minutes. Add the vermouth and cook until evaporated. Add the stock, cream and thyme, season with salt and pepper and bring to a boil.

2 Meanwhile, in a large pot of boiling salted water, cook the gnocchi until they float to the surface, about 3 minutes. Drain well. Add the gnocchi to the mushrooms and simmer, stirring, for 1 minute. Stir in ¼ cup of the Parmesan and sprinkle the remaining 2 tablespoons of Parmesan on top.

3 Broil the gnocchi 6 inches from the heat for 2 to 3 minutes, until golden and bubbling. Drizzle with truffle oil and serve.

WINE *Creamy, nutmeg-scented Sicilian white: 2008 Ajello Majus Bianco.*

RICHARD REDDINGTON

Orecchiette with Sautéed Greens

AND SCALLION SAUCE

chef way

» *When he makes this dish, Richard Reddington of the Napa Valley restaurant Redd fills ravioli with ricotta, mascarpone, arugula, spinach and Swiss chard. He serves the pasta in a sauce of white wine and green garlic.*

easy way

» *Store-bought orecchiette is stirred in the pot with mascarpone, arugula and chard; the ricotta and spinach are left out.*

» *Instead of green garlic, which can be hard to find even during its short season, scallions flavor the sauce.*

INGREDIENTS 4 servings

12 ounces orecchiette
 4 tablespoons unsalted butter
 1 bunch of scallions, thinly sliced
 3 garlic cloves, thinly sliced
 ¾ cup dry white wine
Salt and freshly ground pepper

 2 tablespoons extra-virgin olive oil
 5 ounces baby arugula
 6 large Swiss chard leaves, stems and central ribs discarded, leaves coarsely chopped
 ¼ cup mascarpone cheese

TOTAL 30 minutes

1 In a large pot of boiling salted water, cook the orecchiette until al dente. Drain, reserving ¼ cup of the cooking water.

2 Meanwhile, in a medium saucepan, melt the butter. Add the scallions and garlic and cook over low heat until softened, about 5 minutes. Add the wine and cook over moderate heat until reduced by half, about 5 minutes. Add ½ cup of water and puree the mixture in a blender until smooth. Season the scallion sauce with salt and pepper.

3 Wipe out the pasta pot and heat the olive oil in it. Add the arugula and Swiss chard; cook over high heat until wilted, 5 minutes. Add the pasta, scallion sauce and the reserved pasta cooking water and simmer, tossing and stirring, until the sauce is thick, about 3 minutes. Stir in the mascarpone cheese, season the pasta with salt and pepper and serve right away.

WINE *Zesty, grassy Sauvignon Blanc from France's Loire Valley: 2009 Henri Bourgeois Quincy Haute Victoire.*

ERIC AND SOPHIE BANH
Stir-Fried Noodles
WITH CHANTERELLES

chef way

» *Eric and Sophie Banh of Seattle's Monsoon use as many local ingredients as possible in their classic Vietnamese dishes. They make this noodle stir-fry with earthy wild chanterelles, which are common in the northwestern US (but not in Vietnam). Fresh duck eggs are stirred in during the last few seconds of cooking.*

easy way

» *Fresh organic free-range chicken eggs add practically the same flavor and creamy texture as duck eggs.*

INGREDIENTS 4 servings

8 ounces chow mein noodles
¼ cup canola oil
9 ounces chanterelles, thickly sliced (2 cups; see Note)
Salt and freshly ground pepper
4 large eggs, beaten
2 tablespoons unsalted butter

1 scallion, halved lengthwise and cut crosswise into 3-inch lengths
1 tablespoon soy sauce
1 tablespoon oyster sauce
½ teaspoon chile oil or Chinese chile sauce

TOTAL 30 minutes

1 In a large pot of boiling salted water, cook the noodles until al dente. Drain and shake off the excess water.

2 Heat a wok until very hot. Add the canola oil and heat until shimmering. Add the chanterelles, season with salt and pepper and stir-fry over high heat until softened, 5 minutes. Add the eggs and stir-fry for 10 seconds. Immediately add the noodles, butter, scallion, soy sauce, oyster sauce and chile oil and stir-fry until the eggs are cooked but still slightly creamy, 2 to 3 minutes. Serve.

NOTE The chanterelles can be replaced with an equal amount of shiitake, portobello or oyster mushrooms.

WINE *Lighter-style red Burgundy: 2007 Pierre Morey Monthélie.*

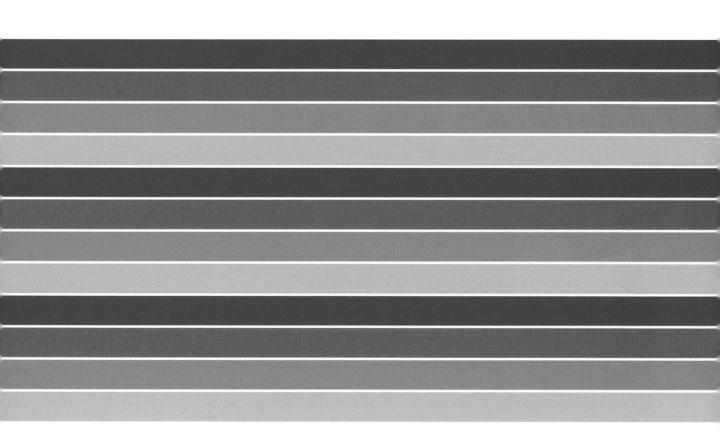

Fish

BOBBY FLAY

Chile-Honey-Glazed Salmon

WITH TWO SAUCES

chef way

» *At Mesa Grill in New York City, Bobby Flay serves his famous spicy-sweet salmon with three different sauces: roasted tomatillo salsa, chipotle-spiced black bean sauce (made from dried beans soaked overnight) and jalapeño crema, a Mexican sour cream.*

easy way

» *The bean sauce—canned black beans, chipotle, garlic and other aromatics—comes together in just 20 minutes.*

» *Plain sour cream fills in for the crema, which can be hard to find.*

INGREDIENTS 4 servings

- 1 pound tomatillos, husked
- 1 red onion, coarsely chopped
- 8 garlic cloves, 2 chopped
- 2 large jalapeños, stemmed
- ¼ cup canola oil, plus more for brushing
- Salt and freshly ground pepper
- ¼ cup fresh lime juice
- ¼ cup chopped cilantro, plus sprigs for garnish
- ¼ cup honey
- 1 canned chipotle in adobo, chopped
- 1 teaspoon ground cumin
- One 19-ounce can black beans with their liquid
- 1½ teaspoons pure ancho chile powder
- 1½ teaspoons Dijon mustard
- Four 8-ounce center-cut salmon fillets with skin
- Sour cream, for serving

ACTIVE 45 minutes   **TOTAL** 1 hour 15 minutes

1 Preheat the oven to 375°. Spread the tomatillos on a roasting pan along with half of the onion, the 6 whole garlic cloves and the jalapeños. Toss with 2 tablespoons of the oil and season with salt and pepper. Roast for about 35 minutes, until tender.

2 Transfer the vegetables to a blender and puree until smooth. Add the lime juice, chopped cilantro and 2 tablespoons of the honey and pulse to blend. Season the tomatillo salsa with salt and pepper and transfer to a bowl. Rinse out the blender.

3 In a medium saucepan, heat another 2 tablespoons of the oil. Add the chipotle, cumin, chopped garlic and the remaining onion and cook over moderate heat, stirring occasionally, until the onion is softened, about 5 minutes. Add the beans with their liquid and ¼ cup of water and cook over low heat for 15 minutes. Transfer the black bean mixture to the blender and puree until smooth. Season the black bean sauce with salt.

4 Light a grill or preheat a grill pan. In a small bowl, combine the remaining 2 tablespoons of honey with the ancho chile powder and mustard and season with salt. Brush the salmon with oil and season with salt and pepper. Grill the fish skin side down over moderately high heat until very crisp, about 3 minutes. Cook the fish on the remaining 3 sides just until lightly charred, 3 minutes longer. Brush the salmon with the chile-honey glaze and grill skin side up until lightly caramelized, 2 minutes.

5 Spoon the tomatillo salsa on plates and top with the grilled salmon. Garnish with the cilantro sprigs and serve with sour cream and the black bean sauce.

WINE *Spicy, cherry-scented Pinot Noir: 2009 Fleur de California Carneros.*

PINO MAFFEO

Roasted Salmon with Tomato Jam

chef way

》 *Pino Maffeo, a Food & Wine Best New Chef 2006, tops his roasted salmon with a Thai chile–spiked fresh tomato jam and flavors his noodle salad with dried shrimp.*

easy way

》 *The tomato jam is made with a quick combo of canned tomatoes, crushed red pepper, vinegar and brown sugar.*

》 *Asian fish sauce—more readily available than dried shrimp— seasons the noodles' curry sauce.*

INGREDIENTS **4 servings**

- 4 ounces rice vermicelli
- ¼ cup plus 1 tablespoon canola oil
- 1 large jalapeño, seeded and minced
- 1 garlic clove, minced
- ¼ cup minced fresh ginger
- 1 large shallot, thinly sliced
- ½ teaspoon Madras curry powder
- 2 tablespoons Asian fish sauce
- 2 tablespoons fresh lime juice, plus wedges for serving
- 1 small red bell pepper, thinly sliced
- 3 tablespoons chopped cilantro, plus leaves for garnish
- 1 small onion, minced
- One 14-ounce can diced tomatoes, drained
- ½ teaspoon crushed red pepper
- 2 tablespoons light brown sugar
- 2 tablespoons rice vinegar
- Salt and freshly ground black pepper
- Four 6-ounce center-cut salmon fillets with skin

TOTAL 1 hour

1 Preheat the oven to 375°. Add the vermicelli to a saucepan of boiling water. Let stand off the heat for 10 minutes, until softened.

2 Meanwhile, in a small skillet, heat 2 tablespoons of the oil. Add the jalapeño, garlic and 2 tablespoons of the ginger and cook over moderately low heat until fragrant, about 4 minutes. Add the shallot and cook, stirring, until softened, 5 minutes. Stir in the curry powder and remove from the heat. Add the fish sauce and lime juice, scraping up any bits stuck to the pan.

3 Drain the vermicelli and shake dry. Cut into 4-inch lengths and transfer to a medium bowl. Add the curry sauce, bell pepper and chopped cilantro and toss well.

4 In a small saucepan, heat 2 tablespoons of the oil. Add the remaining 2 tablespoons of ginger and the onion and cook over moderate heat until softened, about 4 minutes. Add the tomatoes, crushed red pepper, sugar and vinegar and cook over moderate heat, mashing and stirring occasionally, until thick and jamlike, about 10 minutes. Season the jam with salt and black pepper.

5 In an ovenproof skillet, heat the remaining 1 tablespoon of oil. Season the salmon with salt and black pepper; add to the skillet, skin side down. Cook over high heat for 3 minutes. Transfer the skillet to the oven and roast until nearly cooked through, 10 minutes.

6 Spoon the vermicelli onto plates and top with the salmon and tomato jam. Garnish with cilantro and serve with lime wedges.

WINE *Juicy, raspberry-rich Beaujolais: 2009 Jean-Paul Brun Terres Dorées l'Ancien Vieilles Vignes.*

BRUCE SHERMAN

Tuna with Provençal Vegetables

chef way

» *After poaching tuna steaks in a homemade tomato oil, Bruce Sherman of Chicago's North Pond serves them alongside an array of vegetables and homemade pasta.*

easy way

» *Garlic-infused olive oil is an excellent stand-in for Sherman's homemade tomato oil.*

» *A 10-minute sauté of summer vegetables accompanies the fish.*

INGREDIENTS 4 servings

- ½ cup extra-virgin olive oil
- 1 pound zucchini, halved lengthwise and thinly sliced
- 1 red bell pepper, cut into thin strips
- ½ small red onion, thinly sliced
- 4 thyme sprigs
- 4 garlic cloves—2 thinly sliced, 2 halved

Salt and freshly ground pepper
- 1 tomato, coarsely chopped
- 1 small fennel bulb—halved, cored and sliced paper-thin
- ¼ cup pitted kalamata olives, coarsely chopped
- 1 tablespoon drained capers

Four 5-ounce tuna steaks (1 inch thick)

TOTAL 45 minutes

1 In a large, deep skillet, heat ¼ cup of the olive oil. Add the zucchini, bell pepper, onion, thyme sprigs and sliced garlic and season with salt and pepper. Cook over high heat, stirring occasionally, until the vegetables are crisp-tender, about 7 minutes. Add the tomato, fennel, olives and capers, season with salt and pepper and cook, stirring, until the vegetables are tender, 2 to 3 minutes longer. Discard the thyme sprigs.

2 In a medium skillet, heat the remaining ¼ cup of oil with the halved garlic cloves. Season the tuna with salt and pepper, add it to the skillet and cook over moderate heat for 3 minutes, turning once. Cover the skillet and cook the tuna over very low heat for 2 minutes longer; the tuna should still be slightly rare in the center.

3 Spoon the vegetables onto plates. Top with the tuna steaks and the browned garlic halves and serve.

WINE *Rich, creamy white blend: 2007 Henri Milan Le Grand Blanc.*

LIDIA BASTIANICH

Seared Tuna with Tuna-Caper Sauce

chef way

❯❯ *This is an old Sicilian recipe, says Lidia Bastianich. She buys spectacular whole yellowfin for her version, then has someone in her kitchen at Felidia in New York City cut it to her specifications.*

easy way

❯❯ *Home cooks can purchase sushi-grade tuna steaks from a local fishmonger.*

INGREDIENTS 4 servings

One 3-ounce can imported tuna
   in olive oil, drained
¼ cup chicken stock
   or low-sodium broth
¼ cup mayonnaise
1½ teaspoons drained capers
1 anchovy fillet
2 small cornichons
½ teaspoon Dijon mustard
½ teaspoon white wine vinegar
Salt and freshly ground pepper
½ cup plain dry bread crumbs
1 teaspoon chopped thyme
1 teaspoon chopped flat-leaf
   parsley
¼ cup extra-virgin olive oil
Four 7-ounce tuna steaks
   (1 inch thick)

TOTAL 30 minutes

1 In a blender, puree the canned tuna with the chicken stock, mayonnaise, capers, anchovy, cornichons, mustard and white wine vinegar. Season the sauce with salt and pepper.

2 In a small bowl, toss the bread crumbs, thyme, parsley and 1 tablespoon of the oil; season with salt and pepper. Rub the tuna with 1 tablespoon of oil and sprinkle with the seasoned crumbs.

3 In a large nonstick skillet, heat the remaining 2 tablespoons of oil. Add the tuna steaks and cook over high heat, turning once, until golden outside but very rare within, about 5 minutes. Transfer the tuna to a cutting board and cut into ½-inch-thick slices.

4 Spoon the sauce onto plates, top with the sliced tuna and serve.

SERVE WITH Mixed green salad.

WINE *Zesty Vermentino: 2009 Colle dei Bardellini Vigna U Munte.*

MARK SULLIVAN

Cod with Artichokes

AND CHICKPEAS

chef way

» *This recipe is based on* barigoule, *a Provençal dish of artichokes and occasionally mushrooms in a white wine broth. Mark Sullivan of San Francisco's Spruce prepares it with baby artichokes and chanterelles, then serves it with pan-fried cod.*

easy way

» *Frozen pretrimmed artichoke hearts and shiitake mushrooms (cheaper and easier to find than chanterelles) simplify the dish.*

INGREDIENTS 4 servings

- 2 tablespoons unsalted butter
- ¼ cup extra-virgin olive oil
- 1 small white onion, sliced ½ inch thick
- One 9-ounce box frozen artichoke hearts, thawed and pressed dry
- ¼ pound shiitake mushrooms, stems discarded and caps quartered
- 2 carrots, cut into ½-inch pieces
- 2 garlic cloves, thinly sliced
- One 15-ounce can chickpeas, drained
- 1 cup chicken stock or low-sodium broth
- Salt and freshly ground pepper
- 2 tablespoons chopped flat-leaf parsley
- 2 tablespoons snipped chives
- Four 6-ounce skinless cod fillets
- Lemon wedges, for serving

TOTAL 45 minutes

1 In a large, deep skillet, melt the butter in 2 tablespoons of the olive oil. Add the onion, artichoke hearts, shiitake caps, carrots and garlic and cook over moderately high heat, stirring occasionally, until lightly browned, 7 minutes. Add the chickpeas and stock, season with salt and pepper and bring to a boil. Simmer over low heat until the vegetables are tender and the liquid is nearly evaporated, 5 minutes. Stir in the parsley and chives and keep warm.

2 In a large nonstick skillet, heat the remaining 2 tablespoons of olive oil until almost smoking. Season the cod fillets with salt and pepper, add to the skillet and cook over high heat until well browned on the bottom, about 6 minutes. Carefully flip the fillets and cook until they're white throughout, about 3 minutes longer.

3 Spoon the vegetables into shallow bowls and top with the seared cod fillets. Serve with lemon wedges.

WINE *Crisp Grüner Veltliner from Austria: 2009 H.u.M. Hofer.*

JOSE GARCES

Cod with Cockles

AND WHITE WINE

chef way

» *Jose Garces of the Philadelphia restaurant Amada prepares this dish with hake, a relatively hard-to-find cousin of cod. He also uses fresh juice from shucked clams to make the broth.*

easy way

» *Cod can substitute for the hake.*

» *Using bottled clam juice (Look's Atlantic is a good brand) is much less work—and less messy—than shucking clams.*

INGREDIENTS 4 servings

Four 6-ounce skinless cod or hake
 fillets (1¼ inches thick)
Salt and freshly ground pepper
 2 tablespoons all-purpose flour
 2 tablespoons extra-virgin
 olive oil
 2 garlic cloves, minced
 1 pound cockles, scrubbed
 ½ cup dry white wine
 ½ cup bottled clam juice
 2 tablespoons unsalted butter
 2 tablespoons chopped
 flat-leaf parsley
Pinch of smoked sweet paprika
 (optional)

TOTAL 30 minutes

1 Preheat the oven to 375°. Season the fish with salt and pepper and dust lightly with the flour.

2 In a medium ovenproof skillet, heat 1 tablespoon of the olive oil until shimmering. Add the fish and cook over high heat until golden on the bottom, about 4 minutes. Flip the fish. Transfer the skillet to the oven and roast the fish for about 10 minutes, until the flesh flakes with a fork. Transfer the fish to bowls.

3 Meanwhile, in another large skillet, heat the remaining 1 tablespoon of olive oil until shimmering. Add the garlic and cockles and cook over high heat for 1 minute. Add the wine and cook, stirring, for 1 minute. Add the clam juice and cook, stirring, until the cockles open and the liquid is reduced to about ¼ cup, about 7 minutes. Discard any cockles that do not open. Tilt the skillet so the liquid pools to one side. Add the butter to the skillet and swirl until melted. Toss the cockles in the sauce and add the parsley; spoon them over the fish, sprinkle with smoked paprika and serve.

WINE *Bright, melony Albariño: 2009 Nora.*

NOBU MATSUHISA

Black Cod with Miso

chef way

❯❯ *This sweet and silky fish dish from Nobu New York has been cloned at restaurants all over the country. It's fairly straightforward to make, though somewhat time-consuming: Nobu Matsuhisa recommends marinating the black cod in a good amount of the sake-miso mixture for two to three days.*

easy way

❯❯ *The fish marinates overnight in just enough sake and miso to coat. Quickly searing the cod, then finishing it in the oven, creates a beautifully burnished crust.*

INGREDIENTS 6 servings

- 3 tablespoons mirin
- 3 tablespoons sake
- ½ cup white miso paste
- ⅓ cup sugar
- Six 6- to 7-ounce skinless black cod fillets (about 1½ inches thick)
- Vegetable oil, for grilling
- Pickled ginger, for serving

TOTAL 30 minutes + overnight marinating

1 In a small saucepan, bring the mirin and sake to a boil. Whisk in the miso until dissolved. Add the sugar and cook over moderate heat, whisking, just until dissolved. Transfer the marinade to a large baking dish and let cool. Add the fish and turn to coat. Cover and refrigerate overnight.

2 Preheat the oven to 400°. Heat a grill pan and oil it. Scrape the marinade off the fish. Add the fish and cook over high heat until browned, about 2 minutes. Flip the fish onto a heavy rimmed baking sheet and roast for 10 minutes, until flaky. Transfer to plates and serve with pickled ginger.

SERVE WITH Sautéed baby bok choy.

MAKE AHEAD The marinade can be refrigerated for up to 1 week.

WINE *Spicy, full-bodied Alsace Gewürztraminer: 2009 Hugel et Fils.*

SHAWN MCCLAIN

Pan-Seared Halibut

WITH TOMATO VINAIGRETTE

chef way

» *Shawn McClain of Chicago's Green Zebra serves Alaskan halibut with labor-intensive lobster dumplings and a warm tomato-water vinaigrette. To make the intensely flavorful tomato water, he blends heirloom tomatoes with sea salt, then strains the mixture through a cheesecloth overnight.*

easy way

» *As a fast alternative to McClain's tomato water, coarsely chopped tomatoes form a fresh, chunky vinaigrette.*

INGREDIENTS 4 servings

- 1½ pounds heirloom tomatoes, coarsely chopped and juices reserved
- 2 tablespoons minced shallots
- 1 garlic clove, minced
- 1 tablespoon white balsamic vinegar
- 1 tablespoon snipped chives
- 1 tablespoon chopped flat-leaf parsley
- 3 tablespoons extra-virgin olive oil
- 1 teaspoon ground fennel seeds
- Salt and freshly ground pepper
- Four 6-ounce skinless halibut fillets
- 1 tablespoon unsalted butter

TOTAL 25 minutes

1 In a medium bowl, combine the tomatoes and their juices with the shallots, garlic, vinegar, chives, parsley, 2 tablespoons of the olive oil and ¼ teaspoon of the ground fennel. Season the tomato vinaigrette with salt and pepper.

2 In a small bowl, mix the remaining ¾ teaspoon of ground fennel with ½ teaspoon each of salt and pepper. Sprinkle the mixture all over the fish. In a medium nonstick skillet, heat the remaining 1 tablespoon of olive oil until shimmering. Add the halibut and cook over moderately high heat until browned on the bottom, about 5 minutes. Flip the fillets and add the butter to the skillet; spoon the butter over the fillets as they cook, about 2 minutes longer. Transfer the halibut to plates, spoon the tomato vinaigrette on top and serve.

WINE *Fresh, lively unoaked Chardonnay: 2009 Chehalem Inox.*

VIKRAM SUNDERAM

Indian-Spiced Halibut Curry

chef way

» *To season this rich, creamy, deeply flavored dish, Vikram Sunderam of Rasika in Washington, DC, makes his own spice blend with six ingredients, including green and black cardamom, cloves and mace. (Rasika, loosely translated, means "flavors" in Sanskrit.)*

easy way

» *The curry sauce is seasoned with store-bought garam masala, a blend that includes many of the spices Sunderam uses.*

INGREDIENTS 4 to 6 servings

- 2 tablespoons canola oil
- 1 onion, minced
- 2 tablespoons finely chopped fresh ginger
- 4 garlic cloves, minced
- 1 teaspoon cayenne pepper
- 1 teaspoon turmeric
- 1 teaspoon ground coriander
- 1 cup plain whole-milk yogurt
- 1 cup heavy cream
- 1 tablespoon garam masala
- Pinch of saffron threads, crumbled
- Kosher salt
- 2 pounds skinless halibut fillets, cut into 4-inch pieces
- Basmati rice and warm naan, for serving

TOTAL 40 minutes

1 In large, deep skillet, heat the canola oil. Add the onion, ginger and garlic and cook over moderate heat, stirring frequently, until lightly browned, about 6 minutes. Add the cayenne, turmeric and coriander and cook for 1 minute, stirring. Whisk in the yogurt, then add the heavy cream, garam masala and saffron and bring to a boil. Reduce the heat and simmer the sauce until slightly thickened, about 10 minutes. Season with salt.

2 Add the halibut to the sauce and turn to coat. Cook over moderate heat, turning once, until the fish is cooked through, about 10 minutes. Serve with basmati rice and warm naan.

MAKE AHEAD The recipe can be prepared through Step 1 and refrigerated overnight. Bring to a simmer before proceeding.

WINE *Floral Austrian Grüner Veltliner: 2009 Hiedler Löss.*

DANIEL BOULUD

Snapper with Citrus & Fennel Salad

chef way

❯❯ *At Daniel in New York City, Daniel Boulud broils snapper right on dinner plates, then tops the fish with citrus, diced jalapeño and bell peppers. A radish-fennel salad goes alongside.*

easy way

❯❯ *The snapper is broiled on a baking sheet and served with a salad that combines all the bright, crisp flavors of the original dish's components: fennel, radishes, bell pepper, citrus and jalapeño.*

INGREDIENTS 4 servings

- 4 small radishes, sliced paper-thin
- ½ small fennel bulb—halved, cored and shaved paper-thin
- ½ small red or yellow bell pepper, thinly sliced
- 1 jalapeño, seeded and finely diced
- ¼ cup coarsely chopped cilantro
- 1 tablespoon snipped chives
- 1 tablespoon finely shredded mint
- 1 grapefruit
- 1 navel orange
- 2 tablespoons extra-virgin olive oil, plus more for brushing
- 1 tablespoon fresh lemon juice

Salt and freshly ground pepper

Four 6-ounce skinless red snapper fillets

TOTAL 40 minutes

1 Preheat the broiler. In a large bowl, toss the radishes, fennel, bell pepper, jalapeño, cilantro, chives and mint. Using a sharp knife, peel the grapefruit and orange, removing all of the bitter white pith. Working over the bowl, cut between the membranes and release the sections into the bowl. Squeeze the membranes over the bowl. Add the 2 tablespoons of olive oil and the lemon juice to the bowl and season the salad with salt and pepper.

2 Set the fish on a well-oiled, sturdy baking sheet and brush with olive oil; season with salt and pepper. Broil 6 inches from the heat for 4 minutes, on one side only, just until white throughout. Using a spatula, transfer the fish to plates and serve with the salad.

WINE *Citrusy, off-dry Washington State Riesling: 2010 Poet's Leap.*

MICHAEL WHITE

Grilled Fish with Artichoke Caponata

chef way

» *To accompany meaty mahimahi at New York City's Marea, Michael White makes a vinegary caponata (a Sicilian relish) with fresh artichoke hearts instead of the usual tomatoes and eggplant.*

easy way

» *Using jarred marinated artichoke hearts is much easier than trimming and cooking fresh ones. The marinade also gives the caponata an extra boost of flavor.*

INGREDIENTS 6 servings

- ¼ cup extra-virgin olive oil, plus more for rubbing
- 4 tender celery ribs, diced (1 cup)
- 1 onion, finely chopped
- 3 garlic cloves, thinly sliced
- ½ cup prepared tomato sauce
- ½ cup dry white wine
- ¼ cup white wine vinegar
- 8 ounces marinated artichoke hearts, drained and chopped
- ½ cup pitted green olives, chopped
- ¼ cup pine nuts
- 3 tablespoons sugar
- 2 tablespoons small capers, drained

  Kosher salt and freshly ground pepper
- 3 tablespoons shredded basil

  Six 7-ounce skinless mahimahi fillets

TOTAL 45 minutes

1 In a large, deep skillet, heat the ¼ cup of olive oil until shimmering. Add the celery, onion and garlic and cook over moderate heat until just softened, 4 minutes. Add the tomato sauce, wine, vinegar, artichokes, olives, pine nuts, sugar and capers and season with salt and pepper. Simmer until the vegetables are tender and the liquid is reduced, 8 minutes. Stir in the basil and let cool.

2 Light a grill or preheat a grill pan. Rub the fish with olive oil and season with salt and pepper. Grill over moderately high heat, turning once, until cooked through, about 9 minutes. Transfer the fish to plates, top with the artichoke caponata and serve.

MAKE AHEAD The caponata can be refrigerated for up to 3 days.

WINE *Crisp, ripe Italian white: 2009 Casamatta Bianco.*

TRINA HAHNEMANN

Smoked Mackerel Salad

WITH CRUNCHY VEGETABLES

chef way

❱❱ *Denmark-based chef Trina Hahnemann uses smoked mackerel in this sweet-salty salad. She sometimes serves it on a slice of dense whole-grain rye bread.*

easy way

❱❱ *Any flaky smoked fish— like trout or bluefish—can take the place of the mackerel.*

INGREDIENTS 4 servings

½ cup plain 2 percent Greek yogurt
3 tablespoons grated fresh horseradish
1½ tablespoons fresh lemon juice
1½ teaspoons apple cider vinegar
½ teaspoon sugar
9 ounces smoked mackerel or trout, skinned and flaked (2 cups)

One 12-ounce seedless cucumber, peeled and finely diced (2 cups)
5 large radishes, cut into matchsticks
1 large Granny Smith apple, diced
2 tablespoons snipped chives
Salt and freshly ground pepper
1 head of romaine lettuce

TOTAL 25 minutes

In a bowl, whisk the yogurt with the horseradish, lemon juice, vinegar and sugar. Fold in the fish, cucumber, radishes, apple and chives; season with salt and pepper. Top the lettuce leaves with the smoked mackerel salad and serve.

WINE *Bright, lime peel–inflected German Riesling: 2009 Weingut Schneider Laubenheimer Edelmann Riesling.*

Shellfish

TAKASHI YAGIHASHI

Shrimp & Bok Choy Stir-Fry
WITH CRISPY NOODLES

chef way

» *Takashi Yagihashi serves this dish only during his special noodle-centric Sunday brunches at Takashi in Chicago. To make it, he sautés scallops, squid and shrimp in one pan and vegetables in another, then combines them all, topping the stir-fry with crispy deep-fried noodles.*

easy way

» *Shrimp is the star of this stir-fry (the scallops and squid are left out), and cooks along with the vegetables in one pan.*

» *The dish is topped with crunchy instant ramen noodles— no deep-frying necessary.*

INGREDIENTS 4 servings

- ¾ cup chicken stock or low-sodium broth
- 2 tablespoons low-sodium soy sauce
- 1 tablespoon mirin
- 1½ teaspoons cornstarch dissolved in 1 tablespoon water
- 2 tablespoons canola oil
- 2 tablespoons finely julienned peeled fresh ginger
- 1 garlic clove, thinly sliced
- ½ teaspoon crushed red pepper
- 1 large onion, thinly sliced crosswise
- ¼ pound shiitake mushrooms, stemmed and caps thinly sliced
- 1 small head of bok choy (about 12 ounces), thinly sliced crosswise
- 1 pound medium shrimp, shelled and deveined
- ¼ package instant ramen noodles or fried Chinese noodles, crumbled

Brown rice, for serving

TOTAL 30 minutes

1 In a small bowl, whisk the chicken stock with the soy sauce, mirin and cornstarch slurry.

2 Heat a nonstick wok or large, deep skillet until very hot, about 3 minutes. Add the canola oil, ginger, garlic and crushed red pepper and stir-fry until fragrant, about 20 seconds. Add the onion and shiitake and stir-fry until lightly browned and nearly tender, about 3 minutes. Add the bok choy and cook until the leaves are wilted and the stems are crisp-tender, about 2 minutes. Add the shrimp and stir-fry until they are pink, curled and nearly cooked through, about 3 minutes longer.

3 Stir the sauce, then stir it into the wok and cook until slightly thickened, about 2 minutes. Transfer the stir-fry to a serving bowl and garnish with the crispy noodles. Serve with brown rice.

WINE *Off-dry, citrusy Riesling from New Zealand: 2007 Peregrine.*

ERIC AND SOPHIE BANH

Spicy Shrimp in Chile Sauce

chef way

» *At their terrific Vietnamese restaurant Monsoon in Seattle, Eric and Sophie Banh prefer to use wild shrimp for this sweet-spicy stir-fry. The sauce gets richness and a hint of sugar from fresh coconut juice.*

easy way

» *Any large shrimp from the fishmonger will do.*

» *Extracting fresh coconut juice is a lot of work. This recipe calls for packaged coconut water instead (Zico and Vita Coco are good brands).*

INGREDIENTS 4 servings

2 tablespoons sugar
3 tablespoons water
2 tablespoons canola oil
1 small red onion, cut lengthwise into ½-inch wedges
3 garlic cloves, minced
1½ pounds shelled and deveined large shrimp
2 serrano chiles, seeded and minced
1½ tablespoons Asian fish sauce
1½ teaspoons freshly ground pepper
4 scallions, cut into 3-inch lengths
4 tablespoons unsweetened coconut water
Steamed rice, for serving

TOTAL 30 minutes

1 In a small skillet, mix the sugar with 1 tablespoon of the water and cook over high heat, stirring, until the sugar is dissolved. Cook without stirring until a deep amber caramel forms, 2 to 3 minutes. Remove from the heat and stir in the remaining 2 tablespoons of water. Transfer the caramel to a very small heatproof bowl.

2 Heat a wok over high heat. Add the canola oil and heat until just beginning to smoke. Add the onion and garlic and stir-fry until just softened, about 1 minute. Add the shrimp and stir-fry for 1 minute. Add the chiles, fish sauce, pepper, scallions and caramel and cook over moderate heat, stirring occasionally, until the shrimp are pink and curled, about 5 minutes. Add the coconut water and cook until slightly reduced, about 1 minute. Serve with rice.

WINE *Apple-inflected, minerally Alsace Riesling: 2009 Domaine Auther.*

JOSÉ ANDRÉS

Smoky Paella

WITH SHRIMP AND BABY SQUID

chef way

》 *José Andrés serves four different paellas, all cooked over a huge wood-fired grill, at Jaleo in Las Vegas. He prepares this version with lots of seafood, including meaty cuttlefish (a tender, squidlike mollusk), and a house-made fish stock.*

easy way

》 *Baby squid stands in for the hard-to-find cuttlefish.*

》 *Bottled clam juice (Look's Atlantic is a good and widely available brand) provides a nice briny flavor similar to DIY fish stock.*

INGREDIENTS **4 servings**

¼ cup extra-virgin olive oil
1 pound large shrimp, shelled and deveined
Salt and freshly ground pepper
1 cup arborio or Valencia rice
1 tablespoon tomato paste
1 teaspoon hot smoked paprika
1 large garlic clove, minced
1 small pinch of saffron, crumbled
2 cups bottled clam juice
2 cups water
½ pound baby squid, bodies cut into ¼-inch rings

TOTAL **45 minutes**

1 In a large, deep skillet, heat the olive oil until shimmering. Season the shrimp with salt and pepper and add to the skillet. Cook over high heat until lightly browned on one side, 2 minutes. Transfer the shrimp to a plate.

2 Add the rice to the skillet and cook, stirring, until opaque, about 2 minutes. Stir in the tomato paste, paprika, garlic and saffron and cook, stirring, until the rice is toasted and sizzling, about 1 minute. Add the clam juice and water and bring to a boil over high heat. Boil until the rice is still a bit crunchy and about half of the liquid is absorbed, 10 minutes. Lower the heat and simmer until the rice is nearly tender and the liquid is soupy but slightly reduced, about 8 minutes. Stir in the squid, then lay the shrimp on top, cooked side up. Cover and simmer until the squid and shrimp are cooked through and the rice is tender, about 2 minutes longer.

WINE *Crisp, strawberry-scented Provençal rosé: 2010 Château Miraval Pink Floyd.*

ANDREW CARMELLINI

Shrimp in Fresh Citrus Sauce

chef way

» *When Andrew Carmellini makes this dish at Locanda Verde in New York City, he prepares the sauce with blood oranges, tangelos, clementines and tangerines. He sautés the shrimp separately.*

easy way

» *Adding fresh citrus juice (just one kind: grapefruit) to the skillet with the shrimp combines two steps into one.*

INGREDIENTS 6 servings

- 1 tablespoon fresh lemon juice
- ½ teaspoon harissa or hot sauce
- 3 tablespoons extra-virgin olive oil
- 1 large fennel bulb—halved, cored and shaved paper-thin
- 4 celery ribs, very thinly sliced
- 2 navel oranges, peeled and thinly sliced crosswise
- Salt and freshly ground pepper
- 1½ pounds shelled and deveined large shrimp
- ½ cup fresh grapefruit juice
- 2 tablespoons unsalted butter
- 1 tablespoon snipped chives

TOTAL 30 minutes

1 In a large bowl, whisk the lemon juice and harissa with 2 tablespoons of the olive oil. Add the fennel, celery and orange slices, season with salt and pepper and toss. Transfer the salad to plates.

2 In a large skillet, heat the remaining 1 tablespoon of olive oil until smoking. Season the shrimp with salt and pepper and add to the skillet. Cook, stirring once, until just pink and curled, about 2 minutes. Transfer the shrimp to a plate.

3 Add the grapefruit juice to the skillet and cook until reduced by half. Swirl in the butter, then add the chives and shrimp; simmer for 2 minutes, stirring. Top the salad with the shrimp and serve.

WINE *Minerally, citrusy Sauvignon Blanc: 2009 Russiz Superiore Collio.*

RICHARD REDDINGTON

Lemony Shrimp Salad

chef way

》 *At Richard Reddington's Napa Valley restaurant Redd, this dish is composed of two salads: a base of butter lettuce and shrimp tossed in a lemon vinaigrette, and on top, another salad of romaine, tomato, avocado and bacon in a traditional Caesar dressing.*

easy way

》 *Elements of both salads are blended together to create one delicious dish.*

INGREDIENTS 4 servings

- ½ lemon, plus 2 tablespoons fresh lemon juice
- ½ teaspoon black peppercorns
- Salt
- 1 pound shelled and deveined medium shrimp
- 2 tablespoons extra-virgin olive oil
- 2 tablespoons grapeseed or vegetable oil
- Pinch of sugar
- Freshly ground pepper
- 2 hearts of romaine, cut into 1-inch-wide ribbons
- 1 cup grape tomatoes, halved
- 1 Hass avocado, diced
- 2 tablespoons snipped chives

TOTAL 30 minutes

1 Fill a medium saucepan with water. Squeeze the lemon half into the water, then add it to the water with the peppercorns and a generous pinch of salt; bring to a boil. Add the shrimp and simmer until curled and just pink, about 3 minutes. Using a slotted spoon, transfer the shrimp to a paper towel–lined plate. Freeze the shrimp until just chilled, about 5 minutes.

2 Meanwhile, in a large bowl, whisk the lemon juice with the olive oil, grapeseed oil, sugar and a generous pinch each of salt and pepper. Add the romaine, tomatoes, avocado and shrimp and toss. Transfer to plates, garnish with the chives and serve.

WINE *Ripe California Sauvignon Blanc: 2009 Joseph George.*

SANJEEV KAPOOR

Goan Shrimp Curry

chef way

» *Superstar Indian chef Sanjeev Kapoor prepares this shrimp curry in typical Goan style, which means it's tangy, spicy and vibrant. He cracks open whole coconuts and shaves the meat with a box grater.*

easy way

» *Dealing with a whole fresh coconut is difficult; unsweetened flakes from the supermarket are an excellent replacement.*

INGREDIENTS 4 servings

- 3 dried red chiles
- ¼ cup dried unsweetened coconut flakes
- 1½ teaspoons coriander seeds
- 1 teaspoon cumin seeds
- One 1-inch piece of fresh ginger, peeled and chopped
- 4 garlic cloves, chopped
- 1 teaspoon tamarind concentrate (see Note) or 1 tablespoon fresh lemon juice
- 1 tablespoon vegetable oil
- 1 small onion, cut into ¼-inch dice
- 2 jalapeños, halved lengthwise
- 1 pound shelled and deveined medium shrimp
- 1 tablespoon malt or cider vinegar

Salt

TOTAL 20 minutes

1 In a large nonstick skillet, cook the dried chiles, coconut, coriander and cumin over moderately high heat, shaking the skillet, until the coconut starts to brown, about 1 minute; transfer the mixture to a blender or food processor. Add the ginger, garlic, tamarind concentrate and ½ cup of water and puree.

2 In the same skillet, heat the oil. Add the onion and jalapeños and cook over moderately high heat until the onion is golden brown, about 3 minutes. Add the puree and bring to a boil. Add the shrimp and cook over moderately low heat, turning a few times, until just white throughout, about 2 minutes. Remove the skillet from the heat and stir in the vinegar. Season with salt and serve right away.

SERVE WITH Basmati rice.

NOTE Tamarind concentrate is available at specialty food stores.

WINE Vibrant, zesty Albariño: 2009 Bonny Doon Vineyard Ca' del Solo Estate.

JASON FRANEY

Crab Cakes & Curry Mayonnaise

WITH APPLE SALAD

chef way

» *Jason Franey serves his crab cakes at Canlis in Seattle with a curry aioli, a curry powder garnish and two other sauces on the plate.*

easy way

» *Jarred curry paste combined with prepared mayonnaise fills in for Franey's curry aioli.*

INGREDIENTS 4 servings

- ¾ cup mayonnaise
- 1 teaspoon curry paste or powder
- 2 tablespoons crème fraîche
- 2 tablespoons fresh lemon juice
- 1 tablespoon snipped chives
- 1 tablespoon minced flat-leaf parsley
- 1 tablespoon minced tarragon
- 1 large Granny Smith apple, cut into thin matchsticks, plus ½ cup finely diced Granny Smith apple

Salt and freshly ground pepper
- 1 pound lump crabmeat, picked over for shell
- 1 cup *panko* (Japanese bread crumbs)
- ¼ cup canola oil
- 1 tablespoon Champagne vinegar
- 1 cup cilantro leaves

ACTIVE 30 minutes **TOTAL** 1 hour

1 In a small bowl, whisk ¼ cup of the mayonnaise with ½ teaspoon of the curry paste; refrigerate until chilled.

2 Meanwhile, in a large bowl, combine the remaining ½ cup of mayonnaise with the crème fraîche, lemon juice, chives, parsley, tarragon and diced apple. Season with salt and pepper. Fold in the crabmeat, form into 4 patties and coat with the *panko*. Transfer the crab cakes to a lightly oiled baking sheet and refrigerate until chilled.

3 Preheat the broiler and position a rack 8 inches from the heat. Drizzle the crab cakes with 2 tablespoons of the canola oil and broil for about 12 minutes, turning once, until golden and crisp. Transfer the crab cakes to plates.

4 In a medium bowl, whisk the remaining 2 tablespoons of canola oil with the remaining ½ teaspoon of curry paste and the Champagne vinegar and season with salt and pepper. Add the apple matchsticks and cilantro and toss. Serve the crab cakes with the curry mayonnaise and apple salad.

WINE *Crisp, lemony sparkling wine: NV Lucien Albrecht Crémant d'Alsace Brut.*

SHAWN MCCLAIN

Scallops with Summer Squash

chef way

» *Shawn McClain of Chicago's Green Zebra prepares a rich sauce for tender scallops by blanching parsley, tarragon and chervil, then blending the herbs with an egg yolk and olive oil. He adds three-quarters of a pound of prosciutto to the vegetables for four servings.*

easy way

» *Home cooks can skip the blanching (and the egg yolk) and make the herb sauce with olive oil and fresh parsley, tarragon and chives (easier to find than chervil).*

» *Using just an ounce of prosciutto, as an accent, lightens the dish significantly—and it's far less expensive, too.*

INGREDIENTS 4 servings

1 cup flat-leaf parsley leaves	1 teaspoon chopped thyme
¼ cup snipped chives	2 slices of prosciutto (1 ounce), cut into thin ribbons
2 tablespoons tarragon leaves	12 jumbo scallops (about 1¼ pounds)
½ cup plus 2 tablespoons extra-virgin olive oil	½ cup loosely packed Parmesan shavings (½ ounce)
Salt and freshly ground pepper	
1½ pounds mixed small yellow squash and zucchini, halved lengthwise and cut into 1-inch pieces	

TOTAL 30 minutes

1 In a blender or mini processor, chop the parsley, chives and tarragon. With the machine running, slowly pour in ½ cup of the olive oil and blend until the mixture is fairly smooth. Season the herb sauce with salt and pepper.

2 In a large skillet, heat 1 tablespoon of the olive oil until shimmering. Add the squash and zucchini and cook over high heat, stirring occasionally, until crisp-tender, about 5 minutes. Stir in the thyme and 2 tablespoons of the herb sauce; season with salt and pepper. Add the prosciutto and keep warm.

3 In a medium skillet, heat the remaining 1 tablespoon of olive oil until shimmering. Season the scallops with salt and pepper and add them to the skillet. Cook over high heat, turning once, until golden brown and just barely opaque throughout, about 5 minutes. Add 1 tablespoon of the herb sauce and stir to coat.

4 Spoon the squash onto plates and top with the scallops. Drizzle with the remaining herb sauce, garnish with the Parmesan shavings and serve right away.

WINE *Firm, lightly spicy Chardonnay: 2008 DeLoach O.F.S.*

RICHARD REDDINGTON

Scallops with Cauliflower, Capers & Raisins

chef way

» *A cauliflower puree and a drizzle of balsamic reduction accompany Richard Reddington's sautéed scallops at Redd in Napa Valley.*

easy way

» *In place of the time-consuming puree, cauliflower florets brown in the skillet along with the scallops.*

» *A splash of balsamic vinegar is added at the end of cooking as an alternative to the reduction.*

INGREDIENTS 4 servings

½ small head of cauliflower, cut into small florets (4 cups)
1 tablespoon extra-virgin olive oil
12 jumbo scallops (1½ pounds), side muscle removed
Salt and freshly ground pepper
2 tablespoons unsalted butter

¼ cup chopped roasted almonds, preferably marcona
2 tablespoons drained small capers
2 tablespoons golden raisins
2 tablespoons balsamic vinegar
1 tablespoon chopped flat-leaf parsley

TOTAL 30 minutes

1 Bring a medium saucepan of salted water to a boil. Add the cauliflower and boil over high heat until just tender, 3 to 4 minutes. Drain, shaking off the excess water.

2 In a large skillet, heat the oil until shimmering. Season the scallops with salt and pepper; add to the skillet in a single layer and cook over high heat until golden and crusty, about 2 minutes. Turn the scallops. Add the butter, cauliflower, almonds, capers and raisins and cook undisturbed until the scallops are white throughout and the cauliflower is lightly browned in spots, about 1 minute longer. Add the balsamic vinegar and stir gently to coat. Transfer to plates, garnish with the parsley and serve.

WINE *Rich, tropical white blend: 2008 Vinum Cellars White Elephant.*

PINO MAFFEO

Sizzled Clams

WITH UDON AND WATERCRESS

chef way

» *Pino Maffeo, a Food & Wine Best New Chef 2006, prepares this dish with thick, fresh egg noodles and hot chile oil, both homemade.*

easy way

» *Making fresh pasta can be an arduous process. Using dried Japanese udon (and bottled chile oil) saves hours in the kitchen.*

INGREDIENTS 4 servings

- 7 ounces dried udon
- ¼ cup plus 1 teaspoon canola oil
- 2 dozen littleneck clams, scrubbed and rinsed
- 1 tablespoon minced fresh ginger
- 1 garlic clove, thinly sliced
- 1 tablespoon minced flat-leaf parsley
- 1½ teaspoons Chinese black bean sauce
- ¼ cup sake
- 1 bunch of watercress (6 ounces), thick stems discarded
- 1½ tablespoons oyster sauce
- 1 tablespoon unsalted butter
- 1 scallion, thinly sliced
- Chile oil, for drizzling

TOTAL 30 minutes

1 In a medium saucepan of boiling water, cook the udon until tender, 5 minutes. Drain and toss with 1 teaspoon of the canola oil.

2 Meanwhile, heat a wok until very hot. Add 2 tablespoons of the canola oil; when it starts smoking, add the clams. Cover and cook for 2 minutes. Add the ginger, garlic, parsley and black bean sauce and stir-fry for 2 minutes. Add the sake, cover and cook until the clams open, about 5 minutes longer. Pour the clams and their juices into a large bowl. Discard any clams that do not open.

3 Return the wok to high heat and add the remaining 2 tablespoons of canola oil. Add the watercress and stir-fry until crisp-tender, about 2 minutes. Add the udon, oyster sauce and butter and stir-fry until the udon are evenly coated. Return the clams and any accumulated juices to the wok and stir-fry just until combined. Transfer to the bowl, garnish with the scallion and drizzle with chile oil. Serve immediately.

WINE *Zesty, citrusy Sauvignon Blanc: 2010 Casa Silva Reserva.*

ANDREW CARMELLINI

Ligurian Seafood Stew

chef way

» *To make this stew at New York City's Locanda Verde, Andrew Carmellini first blanches peas, snap peas and fingerling potatoes. He adds the vegetables to a homemade mussel broth along with clams, sea bass, an herb pesto and little seafood meatballs made with shrimp, chorizo and scallops.*

easy way

» *The ingredient list is trimmed to the delicious basics, and whole seafood is added directly to the stew, not formed into meatballs.*

» *Bottled clam juice spiked with garlic and spicy chorizo stands in for the homemade mussel broth.*

» *Frozen peas go in at the end of the recipe; they don't need to be blanched—or even thawed.*

INGREDIENTS 6 servings

- ¼ cup plus 2 tablespoons extra-virgin olive oil
- 2 shallots, thinly sliced
- 2 garlic cloves, thinly sliced
- 2 tablespoons finely diced chorizo

Pinch of crushed red pepper

- 1 cup dry white wine
- 2 cups bottled clam juice
- ½ cup water
- 1 cup basil leaves
- 1 tablespoon pine nuts
- 1 tablespoon freshly grated Parmesan cheese

Salt

- 2 dozen littleneck clams
- 1 pound shelled and deveined large shrimp
- 1 pound sea bass fillets, cut into 2-inch pieces
- ½ cup frozen baby peas

Crusty bread, for serving

TOTAL 45 minutes

1 In a medium soup pot, heat 2 tablespoons of the olive oil. Add the shallots, garlic, chorizo and crushed red pepper and cook over high heat until the shallots are softened, about 5 minutes. Add the wine and cook until reduced by half, about 8 minutes. Add the clam juice and water and bring to a boil.

2 Meanwhile, in a food processor, pulse the basil, pine nuts, Parmesan and the remaining ¼ cup of oil. Season the pesto with salt.

3 Add the clams to the soup pot and cook over high heat, stirring occasionally, until they open, about 8 minutes; transfer the clams to a bowl as they open. Discard any that do not open. Add the shrimp and fish to the broth, season with salt and cook until the fish is opaque and firm, about 5 minutes. Return the clams to the pot, add the peas and cook until warmed through. Ladle the stew into deep bowls, drizzle with the pesto and serve with crusty bread.

WINE *Zesty, herbal Vermentino: 2009 Campo al Mare.*

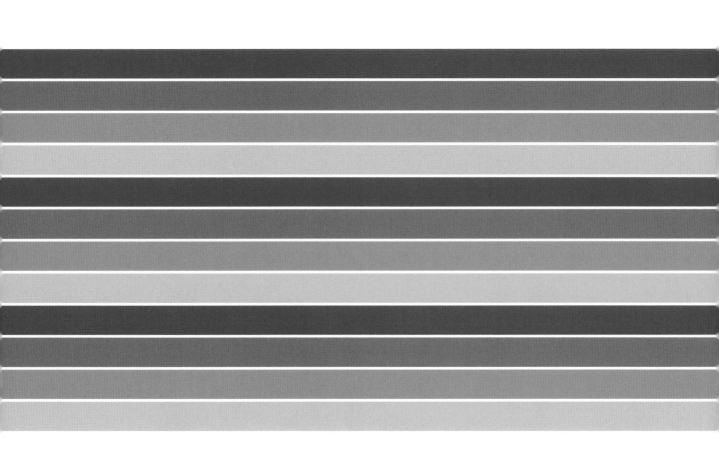

Poultry

MOURAD LAHLOU

Sautéed Chicken with Celery-Root Puree

AND CHESTNUTS

chef way

» *"Chestnuts are a common snack in Morocco," says Marrakech-born Mourad Lahlou. At Aziza in San Francisco, he uses sous-vide equipment to poach fresh chestnuts and chicken breasts, which he serves over a buttery celery-root puree.*

easy way

» *Sautéing the breasts in a skillet creates a crisp brown crust and eliminates the need for any special equipment.*

» *Vacuum-packed chestnuts, which are already peeled and cooked, stand in for fresh nuts.*

INGREDIENTS 4 servings

- 4 tablespoons unsalted butter
- 1 celery root (1¼ pounds), peeled and cut into ½-inch pieces
- ½ cup heavy cream
- 2 cups water
- Salt
- 1 cup vacuum-packed roasted chestnuts, quartered
- 4 celery ribs, thinly sliced on the diagonal
- Pinch of *ras el hanout* (optional)
- Freshly ground pepper
- 1 cup chicken stock
- 2 tablespoons extra-virgin olive oil
- 4 skinless, boneless chicken breasts, pounded ½ inch thick
- 2 tablespoons snipped chives
- 1 tablespoon chopped tarragon

TOTAL 1 hour

1 In a medium saucepan, combine 2 tablespoons of the butter with the celery root, cream, water and a pinch of salt. Cover and simmer over moderate heat for 5 minutes. Uncover and cook until the celery root is tender and the liquid is reduced by half, about 10 minutes. Scrape the mixture into a food processor and puree until smooth. Return the puree to the saucepan and season with salt; keep warm.

2 In a large skillet, melt the remaining 2 tablespoons of butter. Add the chestnuts and cook over moderate heat, stirring occasionally, until lightly browned, about 4 minutes. Add the sliced celery and *ras el hanout,* season with salt and pepper and cook until the celery is crisp-tender, about 2 minutes. Add the stock and cook until the liquid is nearly evaporated and the vegetables are glazed, about 8 minutes. Keep warm.

3 In another large skillet, heat the olive oil until shimmering. Season the chicken breasts with salt and pepper. Add them to the skillet and cook over moderate heat, turning once, until golden and cooked through, about 10 minutes.

4 Spoon the celery-root puree onto plates and top with the chestnuts and celery. Arrange the chicken on top, garnish with the chives and tarragon and serve.

WINE *Floral, full-bodied Viognier: 2009 Cambria Tepusquet Vineyard.*

LIDIA BASTIANICH

Chicken Saltimbocca

chef way

» *Saltimbocca (which means "jump in the mouth") is a Roman dish that's traditionally made with veal, prosciutto and sage. Lidia Bastianich makes her saltimbocca at Felidia in New York City by wrapping boned quail in* speck *(smoked prosciutto) and then pan-roasting it until succulent.*

easy way

» *Quail is expensive and may need to be ordered from a specialty butcher. Inexpensive pounded chicken breasts are a good substitute.*

» *The chicken is topped with prosciutto, which is more readily available than* speck.

INGREDIENTS 4 servings

Four 6-ounce skinless, boneless chicken breast halves, butterflied and lightly pounded
Salt and freshly ground pepper
8 large sage leaves
4 thin slices of prosciutto di Parma
All-purpose flour, for dusting

2 tablespoons extra-virgin olive oil
4 tablespoons unsalted butter, cut into tablespoons
¼ cup plus 2 tablespoons dry white wine
1 cup chicken stock or low-sodium broth

TOTAL 40 minutes

1 Season the chicken with salt and pepper. Place 2 sage leaves on each breast. Top with a slice of prosciutto, trimming it to fit. Press the prosciutto to help it adhere to the chicken. Dust the chicken with flour, shaking off the excess.

2 Heat a large skillet. Add the oil and 2 tablespoons of the butter. Add 2 of the breasts, prosciutto side up, and cook over high heat until nearly cooked through, about 3 minutes. Turn the chicken and cook just until the prosciutto begins to shrink, about 1 minute. Transfer the chicken to a plate; repeat with the remaining chicken. Pour off any fat and wipe out the skillet.

3 Add the remaining butter to the skillet. Add the wine and cook over high heat until reduced by half, 2 minutes. Add the chicken stock and bring to a boil. Cook until reduced by half, 3 minutes.

4 Return the chicken to the skillet, prosciutto side up, and simmer over moderate heat until the chicken is cooked through, about 2 minutes; season with salt and pepper. Transfer the chicken to plates, pour the sauce on top and serve.

SERVE WITH Mixed green salad.

WINE *Fruity, minerally Italian white: 2009 Bastianich Adriatico Friulano.*

MARK SULLIVAN

Moroccan Chicken

WITH MINTY DATE COUSCOUS

chef way

» *At San Francisco's Spruce, Mark Sullivan marinates his North African–style chicken for two days. He serves it with nutty Italian whole-grain farro, which takes about an hour to cook.*

easy way

» *Rubbed with a flavorful spice mixture, the bird only needs to marinate for an hour.*

» *Quick-cooking couscous fills in for the whole-grain farro.*

INGREDIENTS 4 servings

¼ cup plus 2 tablespoons chopped mint
2 large garlic cloves, minced
1 teaspoon finely grated fresh ginger
1 teaspoon sweet paprika
1 teaspoon ground cumin
1 teaspoon ground coriander
¼ teaspoon cinnamon
Pinch of cayenne pepper

Kosher salt
¼ cup plus 2 tablespoons extra-virgin olive oil
One 4-pound chicken, quartered
1 cup chicken stock or low-sodium broth
Freshly ground black pepper
1 cup couscous (6 ounces)
½ cup chopped pitted dates
¼ cup salted roasted almonds

ACTIVE 30 minutes **TOTAL** 2 hours

1 In a small bowl, combine 2 tablespoons of the mint with the garlic, ginger, paprika, cumin, coriander, cinnamon, cayenne and 1 tablespoon of kosher salt. Stir in ¼ cup of the olive oil and rub the mixture all over the chicken. Cover with plastic wrap and let stand at room temperature for 1 hour.

2 Preheat the oven to 400°. In a large ovenproof skillet, heat the remaining 2 tablespoons of olive oil until shimmering. Add the chicken, skin side down, and cook over moderately high heat until browned, about 5 minutes. Flip the chicken. Transfer the skillet to the oven and roast the chicken for about 30 minutes, until cooked through. Transfer the chicken to a platter, cover and keep warm.

3 Pour the pan juices into a heatproof cup and spoon off as much fat as possible. Set the skillet over high heat and add the stock. Cook, scraping up any bits stuck to the pan, until reduced by half, about 5 minutes. Add the pan drippings and season with salt and black pepper; keep warm.

4 In a medium saucepan, bring 1 cup of water to a boil with a pinch of salt. Add the couscous and dates, cover and let stand off the heat until the couscous is tender and the water is absorbed, about 5 minutes. Stir in the almonds and the remaining ¼ cup of mint. Mound the couscous on plates and top with the chicken. Spoon the pan sauce all around and serve right away.

MAKE AHEAD The chicken can marinate overnight in the refrigerator.

WINE *Floral, cherry-scented Dolcetto d'Alba: 2009 Francesco Rinaldi & Figli Roussot.*

ANA SORTUN
Chicken Shawarma
WITH GREEN BEANS AND ZUCCHINI

chef way

» *Ana Sortun of Oleana in Cambridge, Massachusetts, bakes fresh chewy pita bread every day for these Lebanese-inspired wraps. She fills the pitas with spiced chicken that's been braised in beer and garlic, then serves them with* toum, *an intense garlic sauce.*

easy way

» *Using packaged pitas rather than making the bread from scratch saves hours of work.*

» *Boneless chicken thighs roast in the oven in under 30 minutes (no beer-braising necessary).*

» *Cooling garlicky yogurt takes the place of the* toum.

INGREDIENTS 6 servings

1 pound zucchini, sliced ¼ inch thick	¼ teaspoon ground cumin
½ pound green beans	¼ teaspoon ground coriander
½ cup extra-virgin olive oil	6 skinless, boneless chicken thighs
Kosher salt	1 garlic clove, minced
1½ teaspoons ground allspice	1 cup plain low-fat yogurt
1½ teaspoons ground black pepper	2 tablespoons fresh lemon juice
½ teaspoon ground white pepper	Six 6-inch pitas, split horizontally
¼ teaspoon cinnamon	½ small red onion, thinly sliced

ACTIVE 30 minutes **TOTAL** 1 hour

1 Preheat the oven to 425°. In a medium bowl, toss the zucchini and green beans with 2 tablespoons of the olive oil and season with salt; spread the vegetables on a baking sheet. In the same bowl, combine the allspice, black pepper, white pepper, cinnamon, cumin and coriander with 2 tablespoons of the olive oil. Rub the spice paste all over the chicken thighs and season with salt. Arrange the chicken on another baking sheet.

2 Roast the chicken on the lower rack and the vegetables on the upper rack of the oven for 15 minutes, until the vegetables are tender and the chicken is nearly cooked through. Remove the vegetables. Preheat the broiler and broil the chicken 8 inches from the heat, turning once, until crisp and browned, 10 minutes; cut the chicken into strips.

3 Meanwhile, heat the remaining ¼ cup of olive oil in a small skillet. Add the garlic and cook over moderate heat until lightly browned, about 30 seconds. Remove from the heat and whisk in the yogurt and lemon juice; season with salt.

4 Arrange the pitas cut side up on a work surface and brush each round with about 1½ teaspoons of the yogurt sauce. Divide the chicken, roasted vegetables and red onion among the pitas and roll the bread around the filling into tight cylinders.

5 Heat a griddle over moderately high heat. Cook the rolls seam side down until they are golden and crisp, about 2 minutes. Turn the rolls and toast the other side. Cut each roll in half and serve with the remaining yogurt sauce.

WINE *Citrusy, herb-scented Sauvignon Blanc: 2009 Geyser Peak.*

DANIEL BOULUD

Braised Chicken Legs
WITH GREEN OLIVES

chef way

❯❯ *At Daniel in New York City, Daniel Boulud braises duck legs for several hours until they're supertender and incredibly flavorful. Cooking duck with olives is a classic French method: Boulud opts for briny, tangy Picholine olives to offset the richness of the meat.*

easy way

❯❯ *Chicken is cheaper, less gamey and cooks faster than duck (the legs here braise in 45 minutes).*

INGREDIENTS 6 servings

- 2 tablespoons extra-virgin olive oil
- 6 whole chicken legs (¾ pound each)
- Salt and freshly ground pepper
- 4 ounces thickly sliced lean bacon, cut into ¼-inch dice
- 1 medium onion, chopped
- 3 carrots, quartered lengthwise and cut into 1-inch pieces
- 4 small turnips, peeled and cut into 1-inch pieces
- 1 cup pitted green olives, preferably Picholine
- 2 large thyme sprigs
- 1 bay leaf
- 2 cups chicken stock or low-sodium broth

ACTIVE 30 minutes **TOTAL** 1 hour 45 minutes

1 Preheat the oven to 350°. In a large cast-iron casserole, heat the oil until shimmering. Season the chicken with salt and pepper. Add 3 of the legs to the casserole and cook over moderately high heat, turning once, until browned, about 10 minutes. Transfer to a plate and brown the remaining 3 legs over moderate heat.

2 Pour off the fat in the casserole. Add the bacon, onion, carrots and turnips and cook over moderately high heat, stirring, until barely softened, 2 to 3 minutes. Add the olives, thyme sprigs, bay leaf and stock. Nestle the chicken legs in the casserole so they are partially submerged and bring to a boil. Cover with a tight-fitting lid. Transfer the casserole to the oven and cook for about 45 minutes, until the chicken and vegetables are tender.

3 Transfer the chicken and vegetables to a platter; cover and keep warm. Strain the broth into a large measuring cup and skim off as much fat as possible. Return the broth to the casserole and boil until reduced by half, about 5 minutes. Season with salt and pepper. Return the chicken and vegetables to the casserole, cover and cook for 5 minutes to heat through, then serve.

WINE *Spicy, cherry-rich Cabernet Franc: 2009 Bernard Baudry Les Granges Chinon.*

VIKRAM SUNDERAM

Green Chicken Masala

chef way

» *Masalas are Indian spice blends that range from simple mixes of two or three ingredients to complex combinations of 10 or more spices. At Rasika in Washington, DC, Vikram Sunderam's chicken masala recipe calls for about a dozen spices that are added one at a time as the dish slowly cooks.*

easy way

» *Just four distinct spices give this dish its fresh flavor.*

» *Adding the cinnamon, cloves and cardamom all at once cuts back on the cooking time.*

INGREDIENTS 4 to 6 servings

2 cups cilantro leaves	8 skinless, boneless chicken thighs (1¾ pounds), cut into 1-inch pieces
1 cup mint leaves	
1 jalapeño, coarsely chopped	
4 garlic cloves, crushed	1½ teaspoons turmeric
¼ cup fresh lemon juice	½ teaspoon cinnamon
½ cup water	½ teaspoon ground cardamom
2 tablespoons canola oil	⅛ teaspoon ground cloves
1 onion, finely chopped	1 cup unsweetened coconut milk
	Kosher salt
	Basmati rice, for serving

TOTAL 45 minutes

1 In a blender, combine the cilantro, mint, jalapeño, garlic, lemon juice and water and puree until smooth.

2 In a large, deep skillet, heat the oil. Add the onion and cook over moderately high heat, stirring frequently, until softened, about 5 minutes. Add the chicken and turmeric and cook, stirring occasionally, until golden in spots, about 7 minutes. Add the cinnamon, cardamom and cloves and cook for 1 minute. Add the cilantro puree and coconut milk, season with salt and bring to a boil. Simmer over low heat until the sauce is slightly reduced and the chicken is tender, about 15 minutes. Serve with basmati rice.

WINE *Fragrant, juicy Gewürztraminer: 2009 Montinore Estate.*

ERIC AND SOPHIE BANH

Lemongrass Chicken

chef way

›› *Growing up in Saigon, Eric and Sophie Banh ate lemongrass chicken every week. At the siblings' Seattle restaurant Monsoon, they chop whole chickens for the dish. ("The marrow from the bones adds complexity," says Eric.) They also marinate the chicken in a mixture of curry and fish sauce for up to two hours before stir-frying.*

easy way

›› *Boneless chicken thighs require much less prep time than whole chicken.*

›› *Five minutes of marinating is long enough for the chicken to develop a strong curry flavor.*

INGREDIENTS 4 servings

- 2 tablespoons Asian fish sauce
- 3 garlic cloves, crushed
- 1 tablespoon mild curry powder
- ½ teaspoon kosher salt
- 2 tablespoons plus 1½ teaspoons sugar
- 1½ pounds skinless, boneless chicken thighs, cut into 1½-inch pieces

- 3 tablespoons water
- 3 tablespoons canola oil
- 2 fresh lemongrass stalks, tender inner white bulbs only, minced
- 1 large shallot, thinly sliced
- 3 serrano chiles, seeded and minced
- 5 cilantro sprigs
- Steamed rice, for serving

TOTAL 30 minutes

1 In a bowl, combine the fish sauce, garlic, curry powder, salt and 1½ teaspoons of the sugar. Add the chicken to coat.

2 In a small skillet, mix the remaining 2 tablespoons of sugar with 1 tablespoon of the water and cook over high heat, stirring, until the sugar dissolves. Cook without stirring until a deep amber caramel forms, 2 to 3 minutes. Remove from the heat and stir in the remaining 2 tablespoons of water. Transfer the caramel to a very small heatproof bowl.

3 Heat a wok over high heat. Add the oil and heat until shimmering. Add the lemongrass, shallot and chiles and stir-fry until fragrant, about 1 minute. Add the chicken and caramel and stir-fry over moderate heat until the chicken is cooked through and the sauce is slightly thickened, about 8 minutes. Transfer to a bowl and top with the cilantro. Serve with rice.

WINE *Bright, raspberry-rich Beaujolais: 2009 Château de Pizay Morgon.*

TAKASHI YAGIHASHI

Mustard-Glazed Chicken

WITH ARUGULA AND BOK CHOY

chef way

» *When he was training as a chef in Lyon, France, Takashi Yagihashi loved the local Dijon mustard–coated roast chicken. At Takashi in Chicago, he puts his own spin on the dish, slathering chicken with a spicy Asian mustard sauce. He finishes the chicken under a salamander (a restaurant-grade broiler) to give it a crisp crust.*

easy way

» *A salamander is not essential. After searing the chicken in a skillet, briefly roasting it in the oven creates a golden, caramelized glaze.*

INGREDIENTS 4 servings

- 4 teaspoons dry mustard powder
- 4 teaspoons water
- ½ teaspoon mirin
- 1½ teaspoons low-sodium soy sauce
- ¾ teaspoon sugar
- ¼ cup canola oil
- 4 skinless, boneless chicken breast halves (about 6 ounces each)

- Salt and freshly ground pepper
- 2 medium heads of bok choy (about 1¼ pounds), halved lengthwise
- 1 tablespoon rice vinegar
- 5 ounces baby arugula

TOTAL 40 minutes

1 Preheat the oven to 425°. In a small bowl, stir the mustard powder with the water, mirin, 1 teaspoon of the soy sauce and ½ teaspoon of the sugar.

2 In an ovenproof skillet, heat 1 tablespoon of the oil. Season the chicken with salt and pepper and cook over high heat until golden, 2 minutes. Flip the chicken and brush with the mustard mixture; transfer to the oven and roast for 8 minutes, or until cooked through. Transfer the chicken to a cutting board and let rest for 5 minutes, then slice. Wipe out the skillet.

3 Meanwhile, steam the bok choy for 5 minutes. Drain and pat dry. In the same skillet, heat 1 tablespoon of the oil. Add the bok choy cut side down and cook over high heat, turning once, until browned, 3 minutes. Transfer to a platter; season with salt and pepper. Arrange the chicken over the bok choy.

4 In a medium bowl, whisk the vinegar with the remaining oil, soy sauce and sugar; season with salt and pepper. Add the arugula and toss; arrange over the chicken and serve.

WINE *Full-bodied, melony white: 2009 Pine Ridge Chenin Blanc–Viognier.*

PINO MAFFEO

Vegetable & Chicken Stir-Fry

chef way

》 *Green vegetables—broccoli, snow peas and celery—are the main focus of this pan-Asian stir-fry, which Pino Maffeo (a Food & Wine Best New Chef 2006) tops with toasted crushed glutinous rice.*

easy way

》 *The chicken and vegetables in this quick stir-fry are served on a bed of steamed jasmine rice, without the toasted rice garnish.*

INGREDIENTS 4 servings

- ¼ cup canola oil
- 1 medium onion, halved and thinly sliced
- ½ pound skinless, boneless chicken thighs, cut into thin strips
- 1 tablespoon Asian fish sauce
- 1 small head of broccoli, cut into 1-inch florets
- 1 celery rib, thinly sliced
- 4 ounces snow peas (1½ cups)
- 1 garlic clove, thinly sliced
- 1 tablespoon minced fresh ginger
- 1 teaspoon *sambal oelek* or Chinese chile-garlic sauce
- 1 tablespoon hoisin sauce
- 1 tablespoon oyster sauce
- 1 cup mung bean sprouts
- 2 tablespoons shredded basil leaves
- 1 tablespoon fresh lime juice
- Steamed jasmine rice, for serving

TOTAL 30 minutes

1 Heat a wok until very hot. Add 2 tablespoons of the canola oil; when it is nearly smoking, add the onion and chicken. Stir-fry over high heat until the chicken is lightly browned in spots but not cooked through, about 3 minutes. Add the fish sauce and stir-fry for 10 seconds. Scrape the chicken and onion onto a medium plate and wipe out the wok.

2 Heat the remaining 2 tablespoons of oil in the wok. Add the broccoli, celery, snow peas, garlic and ginger and stir-fry over high heat until crisp-tender, 3 to 4 minutes. Return the chicken and onion to the wok along with any accumulated juices. Add the *sambal* and hoisin and oyster sauces and stir-fry just until the chicken is cooked through, 3 to 4 minutes longer. Add the bean sprouts, basil and lime juice and toss well. Transfer to a bowl and serve right away, with steamed jasmine rice.

WINE *Crisp, lime-inflected Vermentino from Italy: 2009 Sella & Mosca La Cala.*

RICHARD REDDINGTON

Stir-Fried Chicken
IN LETTUCE LEAVES

chef way

» *Richard Reddington marinates this Asian-style chicken for at least three hours at Redd in Napa Valley, then sautés it with eggplant, carrots, scallions and mint.*

easy way

» *The chicken marinates for just 10 minutes before being stir-fried.*

» *The vegetables aren't cooked. Shredded carrot, sliced scallions and fresh mint—plus lettuce leaves for wrapping—accompany the chicken.*

INGREDIENTS 4 servings

- 1 pound skinless, boneless chicken thighs, cut into ½-inch dice
- 3 large garlic cloves, minced
- 1½ tablespoons minced fresh ginger
- ½ teaspoon crushed red pepper
- 3 tablespoons vegetable oil
- Salt and freshly ground black pepper
- 1 tablespoon soy sauce
- 1½ teaspoons dry sherry
- 1½ teaspoons Chinese black bean sauce
- 1½ teaspoons sugar
- ¾ teaspoon cornstarch dissolved in 2 tablespoons water
- 1 head of green leaf lettuce, leaves separated
- 1 large carrot, coarsely shredded on a box grater
- 4 scallions, thinly sliced
- ¼ cup shredded mint

TOTAL 40 minutes

1 In a medium bowl, toss the chicken with the garlic, ginger, crushed red pepper and 1 tablespoon of the oil and season with salt and black pepper. Let stand for 10 minutes.

2 Meanwhile, in a small cup, combine the soy sauce with the dry sherry, black bean sauce and sugar. Stir in the dissolved cornstarch.

3 Heat a large skillet or wok until very hot. Add the remaining 2 tablespoons of vegetable oil and heat until smoking, swirling the skillet to coat with the hot oil. Add the marinated chicken and stir-fry over high heat until browned all over, about 10 minutes. Stir the sauce and add it to the chicken, stirring to coat; cook just until the sauce is thickened and glossy, about 1 minute.

4 Arrange the lettuce leaves, carrot, scallions and mint in separate serving bowls and serve with the chicken.

WINE *Lively Spanish red: 2008 Tinto Pesquera.*

ERIC AND SOPHIE BANH

Crunchy Vietnamese Chicken Salad

chef way

» *When they make this zippy dish at Seattle's Monsoon, Eric and Sophie Banh poach whole chickens, then shred the meat. They toss the salad with a homemade scallion oil.*

easy way

» *Using store-bought rotisserie chicken saves time and effort.*

» *The scallion oil is omitted; the salad already gets plenty of flavor from the spicy, vinegary dressing, sliced shallots and fresh herbs.*

INGREDIENTS 4 servings

- 2 tablespoons sugar
- 2 tablespoons plus 1 teaspoon Asian fish sauce
- 1½ tablespoons fresh lime juice, plus lime wedges for serving
- 1½ tablespoons distilled white vinegar
- 1 tablespoon water
- 1 serrano chile with seeds, minced
- 1 small garlic clove, minced
- 1 cup vegetable oil, for frying
- 2 large shallots, thinly sliced

Salt
- 4 cups finely shredded green cabbage (from ½ small head)
- 2 carrots, finely shredded
- ½ small red onion, thinly sliced
- ¼ cup coarsely chopped cilantro
- ¼ cup coarsely chopped mint
- 3 cups shredded rotisserie chicken (from ½ chicken)
- 2 tablespoons extra-virgin olive oil
- 3 tablespoons coarsely chopped unsalted roasted peanuts

TOTAL 45 minutes

1 In a small bowl, combine the sugar, fish sauce, lime juice, vinegar, water, chile and garlic and stir until the sugar is dissolved. Let the dressing stand for 5 minutes.

2 Meanwhile, in a small saucepan, heat the vegetable oil until shimmering. Add the shallots and cook over high heat, stirring constantly, until golden, 3 to 4 minutes. Drain the shallots on paper towels; reserve the oil for another use. Sprinkle the shallots with salt and let cool.

3 In a large bowl, toss the cabbage, carrots, red onion, cilantro, mint and shredded chicken. Add the olive oil and the dressing and toss. Sprinkle with the peanuts and fried shallots and serve the chicken salad with lime wedges.

WINE *Herbal, citrusy New Zealand Sauvignon Blanc: 2010 Wild Rock The Infamous Goose.*

LULZIM REXHEPI

Massaman-Curry Turkey Osso Buco

chef way

❯❯ *Osso buco (Italian for "pierced bone," a reference to the marrow hole in crosscut bones) is traditionally made with veal. When he prepared the dish at Kittichai in New York City, Lulzim Rexhepi used turkey, cutting the legs crosswise to release the deeply flavored marrow. He gave the turkey legs a double curry infusion, first braising them in a curry broth, then finishing them in a delightful red-curry sauce.*

easy way

❯❯ *The drumsticks can be cut by the butcher, or cooked whole.*

❯❯ *The curry infusion is streamlined into a one-pot broth enriched with curry paste, coconut milk and spices.*

INGREDIENTS 12 servings

One 5- to 6-pound turkey breast, backbone removed
¾ cup salted roasted peanuts, plus more for garnish
1 bunch of cilantro, a few leaves reserved for garnish
1 stalk of lemongrass, bruised
⅓ cup thinly sliced fresh ginger
Five 1-inch-wide strips of lime zest
3 shallots, halved
5 garlic cloves
12 cups water
¼ cup canola oil, plus more for rubbing
6 pounds small turkey drumsticks—bottom 2 inches discarded, drumsticks halved crosswise through the bone
Salt and freshly ground pepper
3 tablespoons Thai red curry paste
Two 14½-ounce cans unsweetened coconut milk
¼ cup Asian fish sauce
¼ cup light brown sugar
½ star anise pod
One 2-inch cinnamon stick

ACTIVE 1 hour **TOTAL** 3 hours

1 In a large pot, combine the turkey breast with the ¾ cup of peanuts, the bunch of cilantro, lemongrass, ginger, lime zest, shallots, garlic and water; bring to a boil. Simmer over low heat until an instant-read thermometer inserted in the thickest part of the breast registers 160°, about 1 hour. Transfer the breast to a roasting pan.

2 Strain the broth into a heatproof bowl, pressing hard on the solids. Skim off the fat. Return the broth to the pot and boil until reduced to 8 cups, about 30 minutes.

3 In a very large, deep skillet, heat the ¼ cup of oil until shimmering. Season the turkey osso buco with salt and pepper; add to the skillet. Cook over high heat, turning once or twice, until browned all over, 15 minutes. Transfer to a platter.

4 Add the curry paste to the skillet and cook, stirring, for 30 seconds. Stir in the coconut milk and cook, scraping up any browned bits. Add the turkey broth, fish sauce, brown sugar, star anise and cinnamon stick; bring to a boil. Return the turkey osso buco to the skillet. Cover tightly and simmer over low heat until tender, 1 hour.

5 Transfer the osso buco to a platter; cover and keep warm. Discard the star anise and cinnamon stick. Boil the sauce until thickened and reduced to 6 cups, 15 minutes. Season with salt and pepper. Skim some of the fat from the surface and return the turkey osso buco to the sauce. Cover and keep warm.

6 Meanwhile, preheat the oven to 425°. Rub the turkey breast with oil; season with salt and pepper. Roast for 20 minutes, until the skin is lightly browned and the turkey is heated through. Thinly slice the breast and transfer to bowls along with the osso buco. Ladle the sauce on top, garnish with peanuts and cilantro and serve.

WINE *Vibrant Spanish red: 2009 D. Ventura Viña do Burato Mencía.*

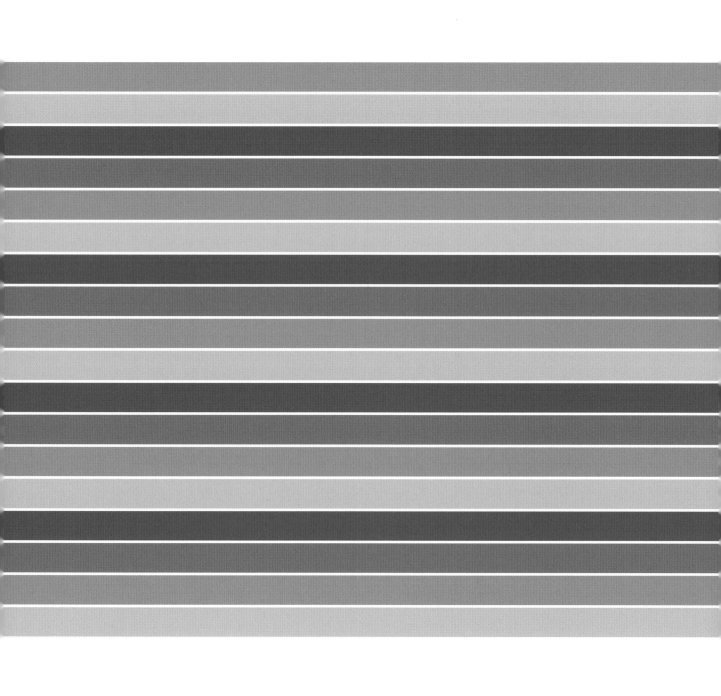

Meat

CHARLES PHAN
Shaking Beef

chef way

❱❱ *Charles Phan's Shaking Beef has been on the menu at San Francisco's Slanted Door since the restaurant opened in 1995. Phan cooks the sweet and vinegary Vietnamese dish— a sauté of filet mignon, scallions, red onion, garlic and a soy-vinegar mixture—in a superhot wok (his stove generates about 180,000 BTU), then serves it with a dipping sauce of lime juice, salt and pepper.*

easy way

❱❱ *Cooking this dish at home (where most gas stove burners put out no more than 15,000 BTU) still results in nicely browned, caramelized meat. It requires only an extra minute or two of cooking.*

❱❱ *Phan's recipe is already incredibly simple. Serving the beef with lime wedges instead of a dipping sauce makes it even easier.*

INGREDIENTS 4 servings

- 1 pound filet mignon, cut into 1-inch pieces
- 3½ tablespoons sugar
- ⅓ cup plus 1 tablespoon canola oil
- Kosher salt and freshly ground pepper
- 3 tablespoons light soy sauce
- 3 tablespoons Asian fish sauce
- 2 tablespoons white vinegar
- 1 teaspoon rice wine (optional)
- 6 scallions, cut into 1-inch pieces
- 1 small red onion, thinly sliced
- 3 garlic cloves, minced
- 1 tablespoon unsalted butter
- 1 bunch of watercress, stemmed
- Lime wedges, for serving

ACTIVE 30 minutes   **TOTAL** 1 hour 30 minutes

1 In a large bowl, toss the meat with ½ tablespoon of the sugar, 1 tablespoon of the oil and 1 teaspoon each of salt and pepper. Let stand at room temperature for 1 hour.

2 In a small bowl, whisk the remaining 3 tablespoons of sugar with the soy sauce, fish sauce, vinegar and rice wine, if using.

3 Heat a large skillet until very hot. Add the remaining ⅓ cup of oil and heat until smoking. Add the meat and cook undisturbed over high heat for 1 minute, until browned. Turn the meat and cook for 1 minute longer. Tilt the skillet and spoon off all but 1 tablespoon of the oil. Scatter the scallions, onion and garlic over the meat and cook for 30 seconds. Stir the soy mixture and add it to the skillet, shaking to coat the meat; bring to a boil. Add the butter and shake the skillet until melted.

4 Line a platter with watercress and pour the shaking beef and vegetables on top. Serve with lime wedges.

WINE *Bright, tangy Beaujolais: 2009 Christophe Pacalet Côte de Brouilly.*

PINO MAFFEO

Thai Grilled Beef Salad

chef way

» *Pino Maffeo, a Food & Wine Best New Chef 2006, adorns this vibrant grilled beef salad with several different types of micro mint and a dusting of toasted rice powder.*

easy way

» *Regular mint from the greengrocer takes the place of the hard-to-find micro mint.*

» *The dish has so many savory and piquant flavors that it doesn't need the rice powder.*

INGREDIENTS 4 servings

Four 4-ounce beef tenderloin steaks
1 tablespoon canola oil
Salt and freshly ground pepper
¼ cup water
2 tablespoons sugar
1 garlic clove, minced
3 tablespoons Asian fish sauce
3 tablespoons fresh lime juice, plus wedges for serving

1 teaspoon *sambal oelek* or Chinese chile-garlic sauce
1 seedless cucumber—peeled, halved and thinly sliced
¼ small red onion, thinly sliced
1 cup mung bean sprouts
½ cup shredded mint leaves
2 tablespoons salted dry-roasted peanuts, chopped

TOTAL 30 minutes

1 Light a grill or preheat a grill pan. Rub the steaks with the canola oil and season with salt and pepper. Grill over high heat, turning the steaks once, until an instant-read thermometer inserted in the thickest part registers 125°, about 12 minutes. Let the steaks rest for 10 minutes before slicing thinly.

2 Meanwhile, in a small skillet, heat the water with the sugar over moderate heat, stirring until dissolved. Transfer to a large bowl. Add the garlic, fish sauce, lime juice and *sambal* and let cool. Add the cucumber, onion, bean sprouts, mint and sliced steak and toss well. Sprinkle with the peanuts and serve right away, with lime wedges.

WINE *Peppery, juicy Zinfandel: 2007 Ravenswood Lodi Old Vine.*

TAKASHI YAGIHASHI

Wasabi Flank Steak

AND MISO-GLAZED POTATOES

chef way

» *At Takashi restaurant in Chicago, Takashi Yagihashi cooks strip steak in a spicy wasabi-horseradish cream. He accompanies the meat with tiny peeled miso-glazed fingerling potatoes and deep-fried salsify (a root vegetable).*

easy way

» *Lean but tasty (and inexpensive) flank steak fills in for strip steak.*

» *The meat is flavored with bottled horseradish and wasabi powder.*

INGREDIENTS 6 servings

- 2 tablespoons wasabi powder
- 2 tablespoons water
- 2 tablespoons drained horseradish
- 1 teaspoon low-sodium soy sauce
- One 2-pound flank steak
- 4 teaspoons canola oil

- Salt and freshly ground pepper
- 1 pound fingerling potatoes
- 1 tablespoon miso
- 1 tablespoon mirin
- 1 bunch of watercress, stemmed, for serving

TOTAL 40 minutes

1 Preheat the oven to 450° and preheat a cast-iron grill pan. In a small bowl, combine the wasabi and water, then stir in the horseradish and soy sauce. Rub the steak with 1 teaspoon of the oil and season with salt and pepper. Grill the steak over high heat until lightly charred, 5 minutes. Flip the steak and spread the wasabi mixture over the charred side.

2 Transfer the pan to the oven and roast the steak for 10 minutes, until an instant-read thermometer inserted in the thickest part registers 135° for medium-rare; transfer the steak to a cutting board and let rest for 10 minutes.

3 Meanwhile, in a saucepan of boiling water, cook the potatoes for 15 minutes. Drain and let cool. Wipe out the saucepan. Add the remaining 3 teaspoons of oil and the potatoes and cook over moderate heat, stirring occasionally, until golden, 5 minutes. Combine the miso and mirin; add to the potatoes and cook, stirring, until glazed, about 2 minutes.

4 Thinly slice the steak across the grain and serve with the miso-glazed potatoes and the watercress.

WINE *Fragrant, lightly tannic Cabernet Franc: 2009 Lang & Reed North Coast.*

MOURAD LAHLOU

Hanger Steak with Charmoula

chef way

❱❱ *This dish was inspired by Moroccan lamb kebabs marinated in charmoula, a tangy sauce of olive oil, garlic, herbs, lemon and spices. At Aziza in San Francisco, Mourad Lahlou likes to use the sauce for hanger steak, which he salts for an entire day before grilling. He serves the meat with cranberry beans and mushrooms cooked in a house-made beef broth.*

easy way

❱❱ *Salting the meat right before cooking rather than a day ahead allows for last-minute prepping.*

❱❱ *Simmering the beans and mushrooms briefly in store-bought broth shortens the recipe by hours.*

INGREDIENTS 4 servings

- 2 cups shelled fresh or frozen cranberry beans (12 ounces)
- 4 thyme sprigs
- 3 garlic cloves, smashed
- Salt and freshly ground black pepper
- 1 packed cup flat-leaf parsley leaves
- ½ packed cup cilantro leaves
- 2 tablespoons fresh lemon juice
- ¾ cup extra-virgin olive oil, plus more for brushing
- ½ teaspoon ground coriander
- ½ teaspoon ground cumin
- 1 pound oyster mushrooms, thickly sliced
- 1 cup beef broth
- 2 pounds trimmed hanger steak
- 2 Italian frying peppers, thickly sliced

TOTAL 1 hour 10 minutes

1 In a large saucepan, combine the beans with the thyme and 2 of the garlic cloves. Cover with water and simmer over moderate heat until the beans are just tender, about 25 minutes. Season with salt and black pepper and let cool slightly in the liquid.

2 Meanwhile, in a food processor, combine the parsley, cilantro and the remaining garlic clove and pulse until chopped. Add the lemon juice and ½ cup of the olive oil and puree until smooth. Scrape the *charmoula* into a bowl. Stir in the ground coriander and cumin and season with salt and pepper.

3 In a large skillet, heat the remaining ¼ cup of olive oil until shimmering. Add the oyster mushrooms, season with salt and pepper and cook over moderately high heat, stirring occasionally, until browned, about 10 minutes.

4 Drain the beans; discard the thyme and garlic. Add the beans and beef broth to the mushrooms and cook over moderate heat until the liquid has nearly evaporated, about 15 minutes. Keep warm.

5 Meanwhile, light a grill or preheat a grill pan. Generously season the steak with salt and pepper and brush with olive oil. Brush the peppers with oil. Grill the steak, turning occasionally, until lightly charred all over and medium-rare within, 10 to 12 minutes. Transfer the steak to a work surface and let rest. Grill the peppers until softened and lightly charred, about 5 minutes.

6 Slice the steak across the grain and serve with the cranberry beans, mushrooms, grilled peppers and *charmoula*.

WINE *Inky, black-fruited Carmenère: 2007 Montes Purple Angel.*

DIONICIO JIMENEZ

Skirt Steak with Creamed Corn

AND POBLANOS

chef way

» *Dionicio Jimenez of El Rey in Philadelphia serves his grilled steak with roasted butternut squash, spiced pinto beans and poblano-spiked creamed corn.*

easy way

» *The butternut squash and pinto beans are left out: The corn-and-poblano mixture alone, made rich and tangy with sour cream, is terrific with the steak.*

INGREDIENTS 4 servings

- 2 poblano chiles
- ¼ cup extra-virgin olive oil
- 1 medium onion, thinly sliced
- 1½ cups fresh or thawed frozen corn kernels
- 1 cup sour cream
- Salt and freshly ground pepper
- 1½ pounds skirt steak, cut into 6-inch pieces

TOTAL 45 minutes

1 Roast the poblanos directly over a gas flame or under a broiler, turning, until charred all over. Transfer to a bowl, cover with plastic wrap and let stand for 10 minutes. Peel, core and seed the chiles, then cut them into thin strips.

2 In a medium saucepan, heat 2 tablespoons of the olive oil until shimmering. Add the onion and cook over moderate heat, stirring, until softened, about 5 minutes. Add the corn and poblano strips and cook until the corn is tender, about 2 minutes. Stir in the sour cream and season with salt and pepper. Keep the creamed corn and poblanos warm over very low heat.

3 Light a grill or preheat a grill pan. Rub the steaks with the remaining 2 tablespoons of oil; season with salt and pepper. Grill over high heat, turning once, until lightly charred, about 6 minutes. Let the steaks rest for 5 minutes, then thinly slice across the grain. Serve with the creamed corn and poblanos.

WINE *Plummy Malbec: 2010 Elsa Bianchi.*

RICK BAYLESS

Carne Asada
WITH BLACK BEANS

chef way

» *At his flagship Frontera Grill in Chicago, Rick Bayless serves this classic Mexican dish of grilled marinated steak with homemade black beans, fried plantains and fresh guacamole.*

easy way

» *The dish is trimmed back to a simple duo of spice-marinated rib eye and canned black beans cooked in chorizo-flavored oil.*

» *Avocado slices stand in for the more labor-intensive guacamole.*

INGREDIENTS 6 servings

- 2 tablespoons vegetable oil
- 4 garlic cloves, minced
- ⅓ cup ancho chile powder
- 2 tablespoons cider vinegar
- 1½ teaspoons dried oregano
- Salt
- Six 12-ounce boneless rib eye steaks (about 1 inch thick)
- 1 dried chorizo (3 ounces), thinly sliced
- 1 large white onion, finely chopped
- Two 15-ounce cans black beans
- Avocado slices and lime wedges, for serving

TOTAL 1 hour + overnight marinating

1 In a small saucepan, heat 1 tablespoon of the vegetable oil. Add the garlic and cook over moderate heat until fragrant, about 1 minute. Add the chile powder, vinegar, 1 teaspoon of the oregano and ¾ cup of water and cook over very low heat, whisking occasionally, until the marinade is slightly thickened, about 3 minutes. Season with salt. Transfer the marinade to a large baking dish and let cool completely. Add the steaks and turn to coat. Cover and refrigerate overnight.

2 Light a grill or preheat a grill pan. In a large saucepan, heat the remaining 1 tablespoon of oil. Add the chorizo and cook over moderate heat until crisp, about 4 minutes. Using a slotted spoon, transfer the chorizo to a bowl; reserve it for another use. Add the onion to the saucepan along with the remaining ½ teaspoon of oregano and cook until softened, about 6 minutes. Add the beans with their liquid and simmer until slightly thickened, about 10 minutes. Season lightly with salt.

3 Grill the rib eye steaks over moderately high heat, turning once, about 12 minutes for medium-rare meat. Serve the steaks with the black beans, avocado slices and lime wedges.

MAKE AHEAD The ancho-chile marinade can be refrigerated for up to 1 week. The cooked black beans can be refrigerated for up to 2 days.

BEER *Crisp, citrusy Mexican lager: Pacifico.*

JONATHON SAWYER

Grilled Steaks with Onion Sauce

AND ONION RELISH

chef way

» *For this dish, Jonathon Sawyer of Cleveland's Greenhouse Tavern marinates steaks overnight in fish sauce and olive oil. He also uses house-made vinegar to make a tangy pickled-onion relish and a silky red onion–jalapeño sauce.*

easy way

» *Marinating the steak for just two hours eliminates the need to plan a whole day ahead.*

» *Rather than pickling the onions for the relish, home cooks can buy jarred cocktail onions.*

INGREDIENTS 6 servings

- 2 tablespoons cracked black pepper
- 2 dry bay leaves, crumbled
- 1 tablespoon Asian fish sauce
- ¼ cup extra-virgin olive oil
- Six 12- to 14-ounce rib eye steaks (about ¾ inch thick)
- 4 tablespoons unsalted butter
- 1 pound red onions, thinly sliced
- 2 pickled jalapeños, seeded
- 1 tablespoon dry red wine
- 2 tablespoons red wine vinegar
- Salt and freshly ground pepper
- ½ cup drained cocktail onions, coarsely chopped
- ¼ cup oil-cured Moroccan olives, pitted and chopped
- ¼ cup torn mint leaves

ACTIVE 40 minutes   **TOTAL** 3 hours

1 In a large, shallow dish, combine the cracked pepper with the bay leaves, fish sauce and 2 tablespoons of the olive oil. Add the steaks to the dish and rub all over with the mixture. Let stand at room temperature for 2 hours or refrigerate for 4 hours.

2 Meanwhile, in a saucepan, melt the butter. Add the red onions and jalapeños and cook over moderate heat until the onions are just softened, 5 minutes. Add the wine and 1 tablespoon of the vinegar and season with salt and ground pepper. Add 2 cups of water and bring to a simmer. Cover and cook over low heat until the onions are very tender, 40 minutes.

3 Uncover the onions and cook over moderate heat, stirring frequently, until the liquid is evaporated, about 10 minutes. Transfer the onions to a blender. Add the remaining 1 tablespoon of vinegar and puree until very smooth. Season the onion sauce with salt and ground pepper.

4 In a medium bowl, toss the cocktail onions, olives and mint leaves with the remaining 2 tablespoons of olive oil.

5 Light a grill or preheat a grill pan. Grill the steaks over moderate heat, turning once or twice, until lightly charred, about 7 minutes for medium-rare meat. Let the steaks rest for 5 minutes, then serve with the onion sauce and pickled-onion relish.

SERVE WITH French fries.

WINE *Rich, blackberry-scented Cabernet Sauvignon: 2009 Wyatt.*

TOM COLICCHIO
Braised Short Ribs

chef way

» Top Chef *judge Tom Colicchio is a master with meat, and his tender, succulent braised short ribs are much in demand at his Craft restaurants. He marinates the short ribs along with vegetables in wine, then discards those vegetables and braises the ribs with fresh vegetables.*

easy way

» *Using the same vegetables in the marinade and the braise means less work and less waste.*

INGREDIENTS 6 servings

- 2 tablespoons canola oil
- 6 flanken-style short ribs with bones, cut 2 inches thick (about 4 pounds; see Note)
- Kosher salt and freshly ground pepper
- 1 large onion, finely chopped
- 2 carrots, sliced
- 3 celery ribs, sliced
- 3 garlic cloves, thickly sliced
- One 750-milliliter bottle dry red wine, such as Cabernet Sauvignon
- 4 thyme sprigs
- 3 cups chicken stock

ACTIVE 1 hour   **TOTAL** 3 hours 15 minutes + overnight marinating

1 In a large skillet, heat the oil. Season the ribs with salt and pepper, add them to the skillet and cook over moderate heat, turning once, until browned and crusty, about 18 minutes. Transfer the ribs to a shallow baking dish in a single layer.

2 Add the onion, carrots, celery and garlic to the skillet and cook over low heat, stirring occasionally, until very soft and lightly browned, about 20 minutes. Add the wine and thyme sprigs and bring to a boil over high heat. Pour the hot marinade over the ribs and let cool. Cover and refrigerate overnight, turning the ribs once.

3 Preheat the oven to 350°. Transfer the ribs and marinade to a large enameled cast-iron casserole. Add the chicken stock and bring to a boil. Cover and cook in the lower third of the oven for 1½ hours, until the meat is tender but not falling apart. Uncover and braise for 45 minutes longer, turning the ribs once or twice, until the sauce is reduced by about half and the meat is very tender.

4 Transfer the meat to a clean shallow baking dish, discarding the bones as they fall off. Strain the sauce into a heatproof measuring cup and skim off as much fat as possible. Pour the sauce over the meat; there should be about 2 cups.

5 Preheat the broiler. Broil the meat, turning once or twice, until glazed and sizzling, about 10 minutes. Transfer the meat to plates, spoon the sauce on top and serve.

SERVE WITH Mashed potatoes, buttered noodles or crusty bread.
NOTE Flanken-style short ribs (short ribs cut across the bones instead of parallel to them) can be ordered at butcher shops.
MAKE AHEAD The braised short ribs can be prepared through Step 4 and refrigerated for up to 2 days.

WINE *Robust Spanish red: 2005 Museum Crianza Cigales.*

DONALD LINK
Spicy & Sticky Baby Back Ribs

chef way

» *Donald Link, the chef behind New Orleans's down-home Cochon, combines eight spices for his rib rub and makes his barbecue sauce with homemade pork stock.*

easy way

» *The number of spices in the rub is reduced to the five essentials.*

» *Canned beef broth replaces the pork stock in the barbecue sauce.*

INGREDIENTS 6 to 8 servings

- 1 cup dark brown sugar
- 3 tablespoons kosher salt
- 1 tablespoon dry mustard
- 1 tablespoon ground fennel
- 1 tablespoon freshly ground black pepper
- 1 tablespoon cayenne pepper
- 1 tablespoon sweet smoked paprika
- 4 racks baby back ribs (about 2½ pounds each), membrane removed from the underside of each rack

- 1 tablespoon unsalted butter
- 1 small onion, minced
- 3 garlic cloves, minced
- 1½ teaspoons dried thyme
- 1 cup ketchup
- 1 cup cider vinegar
- 1 cup beef broth
- ¼ cup hot sauce
- ¼ cup Worcestershire sauce
- 2 tablespoons unsulfured molasses

ACTIVE 40 minutes   **TOTAL** 3 hours 30 minutes + overnight seasoning

1 In a small bowl, combine the brown sugar, salt, mustard, fennel, black pepper, cayenne and paprika. On 2 large rimmed baking sheets, sprinkle the spice mix all over the ribs, pressing and patting it. Cover with foil and refrigerate overnight.

2 Preheat the oven to 250°. Pour off any liquid on the baking sheets, cover the ribs with aluminum foil and roast for about 3 hours, until the meat is tender but not falling off the bone. Pour off any liquid on the baking sheets.

3 Meanwhile, in a saucepan, melt the butter. Add the onion, garlic and thyme and cook over moderate heat until the onion is softened, about 5 minutes. Add the ketchup, vinegar, beef broth, hot sauce, Worcestershire sauce and molasses and bring to a boil. Simmer over low heat, stirring occasionally, until thickened, about 30 minutes.

4 Preheat the broiler and position a rack 10 inches from the heat. Brush the ribs liberally with the barbecue sauce and broil for about 10 minutes, turning and brushing occasionally with the sauce, until well browned and crispy in spots. Transfer the ribs to a work surface and let rest for 5 minutes. Cut in between the bones and mound the ribs on a platter. Pass any extra barbecue sauce on the side.

MAKE AHEAD The roasted ribs and barbecue sauce can be refrigerated separately for up to 4 days. Return to room temperature and broil the ribs just before serving.

WINE *Juicy, berry-rich Zinfandel: 2009 Bedrock Wine Co. Old Vine Sonoma Valley.*

WOLFGANG PUCK

Pork Schnitzel

WITH WARM POTATO SALAD

chef way

» *Wolfgang Puck of Los Angeles's Spago makes his schnitzel by deep-frying cutlets of Kurobuta pork, a deeply marbled heritage meat imported from Japan.*

easy way

» *Boneless pork chops from the supermarket, pounded thin, fill in for the expensive imported meat.*

» *The schnitzel is pan-fried in a shallow pool of oil, not deep-fried.*

INGREDIENTS 4 servings

½ cup white wine vinegar
1½ tablespoons sugar
1 teaspoon thyme leaves
¼ cup canola oil,
    plus more for frying
Salt and freshly ground pepper
1 pound small fingerling potatoes
3 garlic cloves
1 cup all-purpose flour

2 large eggs beaten with
    2 tablespoons water
2 cups *panko*
    (Japanese bread crumbs)
Four 4-ounce boneless pork chops,
    butterflied and pounded
    ⅓ inch thick, or eight 2-ounce
    pork cutlets, lightly pounded
1 cup flat-leaf parsley,
    patted thoroughly dry

TOTAL 45 minutes

1 In a medium bowl, whisk the vinegar with the sugar, thyme and the ¼ cup of oil. Season the dressing with salt and pepper.

2 Put the potatoes and garlic in a pot and cover with water; season with salt and bring to a boil. Simmer over moderate heat until the potatoes are tender, 10 minutes. Drain and thinly slice the potatoes; add to the dressing and toss. Discard the garlic.

3 Put the flour, eggs and *panko* in 3 shallow bowls. Season the pork with salt and pepper and dredge in the flour. Dip the pork in the egg and then in the *panko,* pressing to help the crumbs adhere.

4 In a large skillet, heat ½ inch of oil until shimmering. Add the pork in a single layer and cook over high heat, turning once, until golden and crispy, about 3 minutes. Drain on paper towels. Add the parsley to the skillet and cook, stirring, until crisp, about 30 seconds. Using a slotted spoon, transfer the parsley to a paper towel–lined plate and sprinkle with salt. Serve the pork with the potato salad. Garnish with the parsley.

WINE *Vibrant, lemony Grüner Veltliner: 2009 Hirsch Veltliner #1.*

GEORGE MENDES

Braised Pork with Clams

chef way

» *Pickled vegetables update George Mendes's version of this classic Iberian combination. At Aldea in New York City, he makes his own pickles a day in advance. He also braises the pork and steams the clams in separate pans before combining them on the plate.*

easy way

» *Giardiniera, mixed pickled vegetables sold in a jar, substitutes for house-made pickles.*

» *The pork and clams cook together in an ovenproof skillet.*

INGREDIENTS 6 servings

2 tablespoons extra-virgin olive oil
1½ pounds trimmed boneless pork shoulder, cut into 1-inch pieces
Salt and freshly ground pepper
1 small onion, finely chopped
1 carrot, thinly sliced
1 celery rib, thinly sliced
1 tablespoon tomato paste
½ cup dry white wine
3 cups low-sodium chicken broth

4 thyme sprigs
4 parsley sprigs, plus 2 tablespoons chopped parsley
1 bay leaf
1½ dozen littleneck clams, scrubbed
1 cup jarred pickled Italian vegetables, drained and coarsely chopped
2 tablespoons chopped cilantro

ACTIVE 45 minutes   **TOTAL** 2 hours 30 minutes

1 Preheat the oven to 325°. In a large, deep ovenproof skillet, heat the oil until shimmering. Season the pork with salt and pepper and add it to the skillet in a single layer. Cook over moderately high heat, turning once, until the pork is browned, about 12 minutes. Transfer the pork to a plate. Add the onion, carrot and celery to the skillet and cook over low heat until softened, about 5 minutes.

2 Stir in the tomato paste and return the pork to the skillet. Add the white wine and cook until evaporated. Add the chicken broth and bring to a boil. Using kitchen string, tie the thyme sprigs, parsley sprigs and bay leaf into a bundle; add the bundle to the skillet. Cover tightly and braise in the oven until the meat is tender, about 1 hour and 15 minutes.

3 Return the skillet to the stove. Discard the herb bundle. Simmer the pork uncovered over moderate heat until the liquid is reduced by half, about 15 minutes. Arrange the clams in the liquid, cover and cook until they open, about 6 minutes. Discard any clams that do not open. Transfer the pork and clams to bowls and ladle the braising liquid on top. Garnish with the pickled vegetables, chopped parsley and cilantro and serve right away.

SERVE WITH Crusty bread or fried potatoes.
MAKE AHEAD The braised pork can be refrigerated for up to 4 days.

WINE *Robust Portuguese red: 2007 José Maria da Fonseca Domini.*

ANDREW CARMELLINI

Pork Meat Loaf

WITH TOMATO-CHICKPEA SAUCE

chef way

» *To make the juicy meatballs at New York City's Locanda Verde, Andrew Carmellini mixes pancetta with ground pork loin and pork jowl and nearly 20 other ingredients. He then braises the meatballs in a spicy tomato-chickpea sauce.*

easy way

» *Two meat loaves take the place of meatballs, which require more time to shape.*

» *Most of the meat loaf ingredients (minus the pork jowl and about a dozen other items Carmellini uses) are combined in a food processor. Crushed red pepper adds spice.*

» *The loaves bake in a simple tomato sauce blended with plain store-bought hummus.*

INGREDIENTS 8 servings

Four 1-inch-thick slices of Italian bread, crusts removed, bread soaked in 1 cup milk and squeezed dry
4 ounces sliced bacon
4 ounces sliced prosciutto
1 medium onion, thinly sliced
2 garlic cloves, very finely chopped
4 oil-packed sun-dried tomatoes
1 roasted red pepper from a jar
2 large eggs
2 tablespoons chopped flat-leaf parsley
1 teaspoon chopped thyme
1 teaspoon crushed red pepper
½ teaspoon dried oregano
Kosher salt and freshly ground black pepper
2½ pounds lean ground pork
1 tablespoon extra-virgin olive oil, plus more for brushing
1 cup tomato puree
1 cup chicken stock or low-sodium broth
½ cup prepared plain hummus

ACTIVE 30 minutes **TOTAL** 1 hour 15 minutes

1 Preheat the oven to 350°. In a food processor, pulse the bread, bacon and prosciutto. Add the onion, garlic, sun-dried tomatoes, roasted pepper and eggs; process to a paste. Pulse in the parsley, thyme, crushed red pepper, oregano and 1 teaspoon each of salt and black pepper. Transfer to a bowl and knead in the pork.

2 Preheat the broiler. Pat the mixture into two 8-inch-long loaves. In a large nonstick roasting pan, heat the 1 tablespoon of oil. Transfer the loaves to the pan and cook over moderate heat until the bottoms are browned, 6 minutes. Brush the tops with oil and broil until slightly browned, 8 minutes. Lower the oven to 350°.

3 In a cup, combine the tomato puree, chicken stock and hummus. Pour the mixture into the roasting pan and cook for 30 minutes, or until an instant-read thermometer inserted into the center of one of the loaves registers 180°. Light the broiler.

4 Spoon some of the sauce over the loaves and broil for 5 minutes, until browned. Transfer to a platter and serve with the gravy.

WINE *Robust Aglianico: 2007 Feudi di San Gregorio Rubrato.*

AKASHA RICHMOND

Ham Glazed with Jalapeño
AND POMEGRANATE

chef way

» *At Akasha in Culver City, California, Akasha Richmond prepares a sweet-and-spicy glaze for Thanksgiving ham with house-made pomegranate-jalapeño jelly.*

easy way

» *Store-bought jalapeño jelly doctored with pomegranate juice is a good alternative to homemade.*

INGREDIENTS 12 servings

One 7-pound bone-in, spiral-cut smoked ham
1 cup chicken stock or low-sodium broth
20 whole cloves
One 10-ounce jar jalapeño jelly (1 cup)

1 cup pomegranate juice
2 tablespoons fresh lemon juice
2 tablespoons Dijon mustard
¼ teaspoon cinnamon
¼ teaspoon ground ginger

ACTIVE 30 minutes **TOTAL** 2 hours 30 minutes

1 Preheat the oven to 325°. Place the ham in a large roasting pan and add the chicken stock. Stud the ham all over with the cloves.

2 In a medium saucepan, bring the jalapeño jelly, pomegranate juice and lemon juice to a boil. Simmer over moderate heat until slightly thickened, 10 minutes. Whisk in the mustard, cinnamon and ginger and simmer until reduced to about 1¼ cups, about 5 minutes.

3 Drizzle half of the glaze over the ham and cover with foil. Roast for 1½ hours, basting frequently, until a thermometer inserted in the thickest part of the ham registers 125°. Remove the foil and brush the ham with any remaining glaze. Roast for about 30 minutes longer, until the top is lightly caramelized. Transfer to a platter. Discard the cloves. Pour the pan juices into a bowl and serve with the ham.

WINE *Rich red Rhône blend: 2007 Domaine de la Terre Rouge Tête-à-Tête.*

COREY LEE

Salt-Baked Leg of Lamb

WITH OLIVE OIL POTATOES

chef way

» *For this dish at San Francisco's Benu, Corey Lee uses lamb that feeds predominantly on salty grasses on the Northern California coast. He cooks the meat in a salt crust to echo its naturally briny edge, then garnishes the dish with sea grapes and sea beans.*

easy way

» *Good-quality leg of lamb from a butcher is fine; the meat gets loads of flavor from the herby salt crust.*

» *The esoteric garnishes are simply left out. The tasty, tender lamb needs no accompaniment other than the olive oil potatoes.*

INGREDIENTS 6 servings

- ¾ cup extra-virgin olive oil
- One 3-pound boneless leg of lamb, tied
- Freshly ground pepper
- 5 cups kosher salt, plus more for seasoning
- 2 tablespoons thyme leaves
- 2 teaspoons chopped rosemary
- 2 teaspoons dried lavender leaves
- 8 large egg whites
- 2 pounds Yukon Gold potatoes, peeled and sliced ¼ inch thick

ACTIVE 40 minutes   **TOTAL** 1 hour 40 minutes

1 Preheat the oven to 375°. In a large skillet, heat ¼ cup of the oil until shimmering. Add the lamb and cook over moderately high heat, turning occasionally, until browned, 8 minutes. Transfer to a medium baking dish. Season with pepper; let stand for 10 minutes.

2 Meanwhile, in a medium bowl, combine the 5 cups of kosher salt with the thyme, rosemary and lavender. Add the egg whites and stir until the salt is evenly moistened.

3 Pack the salt all over the lamb in the baking dish, leaving no cracks. Roast in the center of the oven for about 50 minutes, until an instant-read thermometer inserted (through the crust) in the roast registers 120° for medium-rare. Let the lamb rest for 10 minutes, then crack the crust and remove it.

4 Meanwhile, in a large skillet, heat the remaining ½ cup of oil. Add the potatoes, season lightly with salt and cook over moderate heat, turning occasionally, until thoroughly softened but not browned, about 8 minutes. Using a slotted spoon, transfer the potatoes to a platter; season with pepper.

5 Remove the strings and carve the meat into thin slices. Serve with the olive oil potatoes.

WINE *Medium-bodied Italian red: 2009 Calea Nero d'Avola.*

LIDIA BASTIANICH

Rosemary Lamb Chops

chef way

» *Lidia Bastianich makes a rosemary-mint sauce to top the lamb chops at her excellent Italian restaurant Felidia in New York City. She serves the chops with spring vegetables: a mix of sautéed scallions, baby peas, lima beans, zucchini and wilted lettuce.*

easy way

» *In place of the sauce, fresh rosemary is rubbed onto the chops before they're seared, and shredded mint is used as a garnish.*

INGREDIENTS 4 servings

- ¼ cup extra-virgin olive oil
- 4 scallions, thinly sliced
- 1 cup frozen baby peas
- 1 cup frozen baby lima beans
- 1 small zucchini, cut into ½-inch dice
- ¼ teaspoon crushed red pepper
- Salt and freshly ground black pepper

- 6 romaine lettuce leaves, cut crosswise into ¼-inch ribbons
- ¼ cup shredded mint leaves
- 12 baby lamb rib chops (about 2½ pounds), bones frenched (see Note)
- 1 tablespoon minced rosemary

TOTAL 40 minutes

1 In a medium saucepan, heat 3 tablespoons of the olive oil. Add the scallions and cook over moderate heat, stirring, until softened, about 4 minutes. Add the peas, lima beans, zucchini and crushed red pepper and season with salt and black pepper. Cover and cook over very low heat until barely softened, about 15 minutes. Add the lettuce and 2 tablespoons of the mint, cover and cook until the lettuce is very tender, about 10 minutes.

2 Meanwhile, light a grill or preheat a grill pan. Rub the chops with the remaining 1 tablespoon of oil and season with salt and black pepper. Rub the rosemary onto the chops. Grill the chops over high heat for 6 minutes, turning once or twice, for medium-rare meat.

3 Spoon the vegetables onto plates and top with the lamb chops. Garnish with the remaining 2 tablespoons of mint and serve.

NOTE Have your butcher french the chops.

WINE *Medium-bodied Barbera d'Alba: 2009 Fontanafredda.*

JOSE GARCES

Lamb Cutlets with Romesco Sauce

chef way

❯❯ *When he makes this dish at Amada in Philadelphia, Jose Garces butchers the lamb rack himself, then pounds the steaks superthin. Next he rolls the meat around a filling made with whipped goat cheese, crème fraîche and herbs. He serves the finished meat rolls with homemade* romesco *sauce, a classic Spanish blend of tomatoes, almonds and roasted red peppers.*

easy way

❯❯ *An alternative to making meat rolls: coating the pounded lamb steaks in bread crumbs and pan-frying until crisp.*

❯❯ *The cutlets are topped with a tangy* romesco *sauce made from jarred red peppers and then sprinkled with goat cheese and chopped fresh herbs.*

INGREDIENTS 4 servings

- 1½ pounds boneless lamb leg steaks, cut ½ inch thick and lightly pounded
- Salt and freshly ground pepper
- ½ cup all-purpose flour
- 2 large eggs, beaten
- 1½ cups *panko* (Japanese bread crumbs)
- 1 medium tomato, seeded and chopped
- 1 roasted red pepper from a jar
- 1 garlic clove
- ¼ cup salted roasted almonds
- 2 tablespoons red wine vinegar
- Pinch of sugar
- ¼ cup extra-virgin olive oil, plus more for frying
- 2 ounces fresh goat cheese, crumbled (¼ cup)
- 2 tablespoons snipped chives
- 2 tablespoons coarsely chopped flat-leaf parsley

TOTAL 40 minutes

1 Season the lamb with salt and pepper. Put the flour, eggs and *panko* in 3 shallow bowls; season each with salt and pepper. Dredge the lamb in the flour, then dip in the eggs and coat with *panko*. Transfer the lamb to a plate.

2 In a blender, combine the tomato, roasted pepper, garlic, almonds, vinegar and sugar and process until smooth. With the machine on, add the ¼ cup of olive oil in a thin stream and blend until creamy. Season the *romesco* sauce with salt and pepper.

3 In a large skillet, heat ¼ inch of olive oil until shimmering. Add the breaded lamb cutlets and cook over moderately high heat, turning once, until golden and crisp, about 7 minutes. Drain on paper towels and transfer to plates. Spoon some of the *romesco* sauce over the lamb and garnish with the goat cheese, chives and parsley. Serve the remaining sauce on the side.

WINE *Ripe, blackberry-rich Garnacha: 2008 Vega Sindoa El Chaparral.*

JASON FRANEY

Lamb Ragout

WITH OLIVES AND PEPPERS

chef way

》 *Seattle chef Jason Franey serves the lamb in his dish at Canlis two ways: in a ragout and as chops. Two sides—potato puree and Israeli couscous—accompany the lamb.*

easy way

》 *The lamb ragout and the couscous are amazing on their own, and half the work to make.*

INGREDIENTS 6 servings

¼ cup canola oil
4 pounds boneless lamb shoulder, cut into 2-inch chunks
Salt and freshly ground black pepper
2 large white onions, coarsely chopped
4 celery ribs, coarsely chopped
3 carrots, coarsely chopped
¼ cup tomato paste
1 cup dry red wine
10 cups water
1 tablespoon unsalted butter, softened
1 tablespoon all-purpose flour
¾ cup sliced pitted Picholine olives
¾ cup sliced roasted red peppers
2 tablespoons chopped tarragon
2 cups Israeli couscous

ACTIVE 45 minutes   **TOTAL** 3 hours 30 minutes

1 Preheat the oven to 250°. In a large enameled cast-iron casserole, heat the oil until shimmering. Season the lamb with salt and pepper and add it to the casserole. Cook over moderately high heat, turning the pieces once or twice, until deeply browned, 15 to 18 minutes. Transfer the lamb to a platter.

2 Add the onions, celery and carrots to the casserole. Cover and cook over low heat just until softened, about 5 minutes. Add the tomato paste and cook over moderately high heat, stirring, until the paste is lightly browned, about 5 minutes. Add the wine and cook, scraping up any browned bits, until nearly evaporated, about 5 minutes. Add the water, season with salt and bring to a boil. Return the lamb and any accumulated juices to the casserole. Cover and braise in the oven for about 2½ hours, until tender.

3 Transfer the lamb to the platter. Remove any fat and gristle and coarsely shred the meat. Strain the broth and discard the solids. Skim the fat from the surface of the broth. Return the broth to the casserole and boil until reduced to 4 cups, about 30 minutes.

4 In a small bowl, mix the butter with the flour to form a paste; whisk it into the broth and simmer until thickened, about 5 minutes. Return the lamb to the sauce. Add the olives, red peppers and tarragon and keep warm.

5 Bring a large pot of salted water to a boil. Add the couscous and cook until tender, about 5 minutes. Drain the couscous and transfer to shallow bowls. Spoon the lamb ragout over the couscous and serve.

WINE Red-berried Syrah blend: 2009 Château des Tours Côtes-du-Rhône Rouge.

DANIEL BOULUD

Blanquette de Veau

chef way

» *Veal stock flavors Daniel Boulud's version of this classic creamy veal stew at New York City's Daniel. ("Blanquette" comes from the French word* blanc, *which means "white.") Boulud sometimes adds sweetbreads and finishes the dish with shavings of decadent black truffle.*

easy way

» *Store-bought vegetable broth— or even salted water—can replace the veal stock, which would take hours to make from scratch and is tough to find in cans.*

» *The sweetbreads and truffle shavings are omitted. The vegetables, herbs, spices and cream are rich and flavorful by themselves.*

INGREDIENTS 4 servings

- 2 pounds trimmed boneless veal shoulder, cut into 2-inch chunks
- 1½ quarts low-sodium vegetable broth
- 3 parsley stems, plus 2 tablespoons chopped parsley
- 2 thyme sprigs
- 1 bay leaf
- ½ teaspoon black peppercorns
- ½ teaspoon coriander seeds
- 1 small white onion stuck with 6 cloves
- 1 leek, white part only, halved and cut into 1-inch pieces

- 1 large carrot, cut into 1-inch pieces
- 1 medium celery rib, cut into 1-inch pieces
- 1 cup heavy cream
- 1 tablespoon unsalted butter, softened
- 1 tablespoon all-purpose flour
- 1 tablespoon fresh lemon juice

Pinch of cayenne pepper

Salt and freshly ground black pepper
- 2 tablespoons minced chives

ACTIVE 40 minutes   **TOTAL** 2 hours 20 minutes

1 In a medium enameled cast-iron casserole, cover the veal with the broth and bring to a simmer over moderately high heat. Tie the parsley stems, thyme sprigs, bay leaf, peppercorns and coriander seeds in a piece of cheesecloth and add the bundle to the casserole along with the onion. Simmer over low heat for 1 hour, skimming occasionally. Add the leek, carrot and celery and simmer until the veal is tender, 45 minutes longer. Drain the meat and vegetables, reserving the broth. Discard the bundle and onion. Cover the meat and vegetables to keep them from drying out.

2 Return the broth to the casserole; you should have about 4 cups. Boil the broth over high heat until reduced by half, about 8 minutes. Add the heavy cream and simmer over moderately low heat until reduced by a third, about 6 minutes.

3 In a small bowl, blend the butter and flour to form a paste. Whisk ½ cup of the hot liquid into the paste until smooth, then whisk into the remaining liquid in the casserole. Simmer over moderate heat, whisking often, until the sauce is thickened and no floury taste remains, about 5 minutes. Add the veal and vegetables along with the lemon juice and cayenne and simmer over low heat until the meat is hot. Season the stew with salt and black pepper. Stir in the chopped parsley and chives and serve.

WINE *Minerally Chardonnay: 2009 Calera Central Coast.*

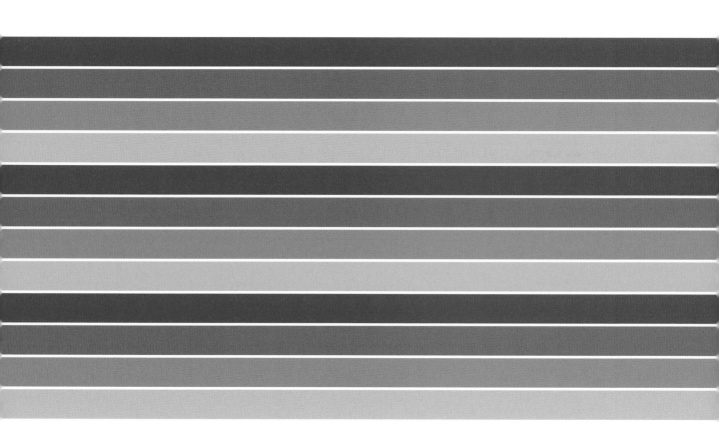

Vegetable

s & Sides

TAKASHI YAGIHASHI

Tofu Casserole

chef way

⟩⟩ *At Takashi restaurant in Chicago, Takashi Yagihashi sets out a pot of broth containing tofu, enoki and shiitake mushrooms and Asian greens like* kombu *(a seaweed) and* shungiku *(edible chrysanthemum leaves). Diners pluck out the ingredients they want, then dip them in bowls of soy, mirin and yuzu juice, a tart Japanese citrus juice.*

easy way

⟩⟩ *Supermarket ingredients stand in for specialty items, and everything—soy and mirin included—goes right in the pot.*

INGREDIENTS 4 servings

- 2 teaspoons instant dashi powder (see Note)
- 4 cups water
- 2 teaspoons finely grated fresh ginger
- ¼ pound shiitake mushrooms, stemmed and caps thinly sliced
- ½ cup shelled edamame (3 ounces)
- One 14-ounce package firm silken tofu, cut into 1-inch cubes
- 8 water chestnuts, thinly sliced
- 5 ounces baby spinach
- 2 tablespoons low-sodium soy sauce
- 2 tablespoons mirin
- 1 teaspoon fresh lemon juice
- 1 scallion, thinly sliced
- 4 teaspoons bonito flakes, optional (see Note)

TOTAL 30 minutes

In a large saucepan, bring the dashi and water to a simmer. Add the ginger, shiitake, edamame, tofu and water chestnuts and simmer over moderate heat for 5 minutes. Add the spinach, soy sauce, mirin and lemon juice and stir just until the spinach is wilted. Serve in bowls with the scallion and bonito flakes.

NOTE Instant dashi is Japanese stock made from bonito flakes (dried tuna shavings) and seaweed. Look for dashi and bonito flakes in the Asian section of supermarkets.

PINO MAFFEO

Crispy Tofu with Noodles

chef way

» *Pino Maffeo, a Food & Wine Best New Chef 2006, coats tofu in tempura batter, then deep-fries it. He garnishes the finished dish with lily buds (unopened flowers of daylilies), which have a slightly sweet, musky flavor.*

easy way

» *The tofu is tossed with packaged* panko *(Japanese bread crumbs), then stir-fried in a wok until crispy.*

» *Mushrooms add plenty of earthiness to the dish—the lily bud garnish can be omitted.*

INGREDIENTS 4 servings

- 7 ounces dried udon
- ½ cup plus 1 teaspoon canola oil
- 1 cup *panko* (Japanese bread crumbs)
- 6 ounces firm tofu, cut into 1-inch squares
- 1 egg yolk
- ¾ pound mixed mushrooms, such as oyster, hen-of-the-woods and stemmed shiitake, thickly sliced
- 1 tablespoon minced fresh ginger
- 1 garlic clove, minced
- ¾ pound baby bok choy, cut into ¾-inch pieces
- 2 tablespoons oyster sauce
- 1½ tablespoons hoisin sauce

TOTAL 35 minutes

1 Bring a saucepan of water to a boil. Add the udon and cook until tender, 5 minutes; drain. Toss with 1 teaspoon of the canola oil.

2 Meanwhile, put the *panko* in a large, resealable plastic bag and crush into fine crumbs. In a shallow bowl, gently toss the tofu with the egg yolk. Transfer the tofu to the bag and coat with the *panko*.

3 Heat the remaining ½ cup of oil in a wok until just smoking. Add the tofu and stir-fry over high heat until crisp, 2 to 3 minutes. Using a slotted spoon, transfer to a paper towel–lined plate.

4 Pour off all but ¼ cup of the oil and return the wok to high heat. Add the mushrooms and stir-fry until lightly browned, about 3 minutes. Add the ginger, garlic and bok choy and stir-fry for 5 minutes. Add the udon and oyster and hoisin sauces and stir-fry for 2 minutes. Add the tofu and toss. Transfer to a bowl and serve.

WINE *Rhône white: 2009 Jean-Luc Colombo Les Figuières Côtes-du-Rhône.*

JERRY TRAUNFELD

White Beans with Onion Confit

¼ cup plus 2 tablespoons extra-virgin olive oil
2 large onions, thinly sliced
10 garlic cloves, thinly sliced
1 scant tablespoon chopped rosemary
¼ teaspoon crushed red pepper
Kosher salt and freshly ground black pepper

Two 15-ounce cans cannellini beans, drained and rinsed
2 tablespoons chopped flat-leaf parsley
1 cup water
¼ cup freshly grated Parmigiano-Reggiano cheese

TOTAL 45 minutes

chef way

❯❯ *To make this dish, Jerry Traunfeld of Seattle's Poppy cooks onions and garlic very slowly in a generous amount of oil until they're sweet and caramelized, then mixes them into boiled cranberry or corona beans (which he's soaked and cooked ahead of time). He finishes the dish with fresh herbs from the restaurant's garden.*

easy way

❯❯ *Using canned cannellini beans eliminates the need for soaking and cooking dried beans.*

❯❯ *All the ingredients cook together in a single saucepan.*

In a large saucepan, heat the olive oil until shimmering. Add the onions, garlic, rosemary and crushed red pepper and season with salt and black pepper. Cover and cook over moderately high heat, stirring occasionally, until just softened, about 5 minutes. Uncover and cook over moderately low heat, stirring occasionally, until the onions are very soft and lightly caramelized, about 15 minutes longer. Stir in the beans, parsley and water and simmer until stewy, about 5 minutes. Stir in the cheese and season with salt and black pepper. Serve warm or at room temperature.

SERVE WITH Crusty bread.
MAKE AHEAD The cooked beans can be refrigerated overnight.

WINE *Citrusy Albariño: 2009 Santiago Ruiz.*

SANJEEV KAPOOR

Chickpeas in Spicy Tomato Gravy

chef way

» *For this classic Punjabi chickpea dish known as* masaledar chholay, *superstar Indian chef Sanjeev Kapoor toasts cumin seeds in a pan until they're quite brown, then grinds them to a fine powder with a mortar and pestle.*

easy way

» *There's no need for a mortar and pestle: The chickpeas get terrific flavor from preground cumin, coriander and cayenne.*

INGREDIENTS 4 to 6 servings

- 8 garlic cloves, chopped
- 2 jalapeños, chopped
- One 2-inch piece of fresh ginger, peeled and chopped
- ¼ cup vegetable oil
- 3 onions, cut into ¼-inch dice
- 2 tablespoons ground cumin
- 1 tablespoon ground coriander
- ¾ teaspoon cayenne pepper
- 1½ cups canned diced tomatoes
- Two 15-ounce cans chickpeas, drained and rinsed
- 2 cups water
- Salt
- 2 tablespoons cilantro leaves

TOTAL 35 minutes

1 In a mini food processor, combine the garlic, jalapeños and ginger and process to a paste.

2 In a large nonstick skillet, heat the oil. Add the onions and cook over moderately high heat until sizzling, about 3 minutes. Reduce the heat to moderate and cook, stirring occasionally, until the onions are browned, about 7 minutes. Add the garlic paste and cook, stirring, until fragrant, about 2 minutes. Add the cumin, coriander and cayenne and cook, stirring, for 1 minute. Add the tomatoes and simmer over moderate heat until thickened, about 6 minutes. Add the chickpeas and water and simmer until the chickpeas are flavored with the gravy, about 8 minutes. Season the chickpeas with salt, garnish with the cilantro and serve.

SERVE WITH Yogurt and naan.

WINE *Concentrated, fruity Italian rosato: 2010 Di Giovanna Gerbino Rosato di Nerello Mascalese.*

VIKRAM SUNDERAM

Three-Bean Dal

chef way

» *To make this soothing, creamy dish, Vikram Sunderam of Rasika in Washington, DC, soaks three different legumes overnight: red kidney beans, whole black lentils and split dried chickpeas.*

easy way

» *Quick-cooking yellow split peas and canned beans make this recipe fast but still satisfying.*

INGREDIENTS 4 to 6 servings

 1 cup yellow split peas (7 ounces)
Kosher salt
 3 tablespoons canola oil
 2 tablespoons minced
   fresh ginger
 2 large garlic cloves, minced
 1 jalapeño, seeded and minced
 1 teaspoon cumin seeds
 ½ teaspoon cayenne pepper
 1 small tomato, chopped
 1 tablespoon tomato paste
 ¾ cup heavy cream
 2 tablespoons unsalted butter
 ½ cup water
One 15-ounce can chickpeas,
   drained and rinsed
One 15-ounce can red kidney beans,
   drained and rinsed
Basmati rice and warm naan,
   for serving

ACTIVE 15 minutes   **TOTAL** 1 hour 20 minutes

1 In a medium saucepan, bring 6 cups of water to a boil. Add the split peas and a generous pinch of salt and boil until just beginning to break down, about 50 minutes. Drain well.

2 Meanwhile, in a large, deep skillet, heat the oil. Add the ginger, garlic, jalapeño, cumin and cayenne and cook over moderate heat until softened, about 6 minutes. Add the tomato and tomato paste and cook until the tomato is slightly broken down, about 5 minutes. Add the cream, butter and water and bring to a boil. Stir in the yellow split peas, chickpeas and kidney beans and season with salt. Simmer over low heat until thickened, about 15 minutes. Serve with basmati rice and naan.

MAKE AHEAD The recipe can be refrigerated for up to 3 days.

SHAWN MCCLAIN

Bok Choy with Black Bean Sauce

chef way

» *Shawn McClain of Chicago's Green Zebra uses Chinese fermented black beans, homemade chicken stock and peanut oil to flavor his chile-spiked stir-fry.*

easy way

» *Fermented black beans may require some hunting to find; the more ubiquitous jarred Chinese black bean sauce is an excellent substitute.*

» *Store-bought chicken broth takes the place of homemade.*

» *Peanut oil is dropped in favor of vegetable oil, a pantry staple that's lower in saturated fat.*

INGREDIENTS 4 servings

- 1 tablespoon vegetable oil
- 1 garlic clove, minced
- 1 tablespoon minced fresh ginger
- 2 scallions, thinly sliced
- 2 tablespoons black bean sauce
- 1 tablespoon dry sherry
- ½ cup chicken broth
- ¼ teaspoon Asian chile paste
- 1¼ pounds baby bok choy, quartered lengthwise
- 1 bunch of watercress (6 ounces), thick stems discarded
- 1 teaspoon cornstarch mixed with 1 tablespoon water

Steamed rice, for serving

TOTAL 30 minutes

1 In a large skillet, heat the oil until shimmering. Add the garlic, ginger and scallions and cook over moderate heat until softened, about 2 minutes. Add the black bean sauce, sherry, chicken broth and chile paste, bring to a boil and simmer the sauce for 1 minute.

2 Meanwhile, place the bok choy in a steamer and steam until crisp-tender, about 3 minutes. Add the watercress to the steamer and cook just until it wilts, about 1 minute longer.

3 Add the bok choy and watercress to the skillet with the sauce. Stir the cornstarch mixture; add it to the skillet and stir-fry over high heat until the sauce is thickened, about 1 minute. Transfer the vegetables to a bowl and serve with rice.

ANDREW CARMELLINI

Spicy Braised Escarole

chef way

» *At Locanda Verde in New York City, Andrew Carmellini prepares this dish with homemade bread crumbs and intensely flavorful Sicilian oregano.*

easy way

» *Packaged* panko *mixed with Parmesan tops the spicy greens.*

» *Domestic fresh oregano fills in for hard-to-find Sicilian.*

INGREDIENTS 6 servings

- 3 tablespoons extra-virgin olive oil
- ¼ pound thickly sliced soppressata, cut into ¼-inch dice
- 2 garlic cloves, minced
- ½ teaspoon crushed red pepper
- 4 heads of escarole (2½ pounds), dark outer leaves removed, inner leaves coarsely chopped
- One 14-ounce can diced tomatoes
- 1 tablespoon minced fresh oregano
- Salt and freshly ground black pepper
- ¼ cup *panko* (Japanese bread crumbs)
- 2 tablespoons freshly grated Parmesan cheese

TOTAL 35 minutes

1 In a large soup pot, heat 2 tablespoons of the oil. Add the soppressata, garlic and crushed red pepper and cook over high heat, stirring, until the garlic is golden, about 2 minutes. Add the escarole in batches, allowing each batch to wilt before adding more. Add the tomatoes and oregano, season with salt and black pepper and bring to a boil. Cook over low heat until the escarole is tender, 15 minutes; transfer to a bowl.

2 Meanwhile, in a small skillet, heat the remaining 1 tablespoon of olive oil. Add the *panko* and cook over moderate heat, stirring, until golden, about 1 minute. Off the heat, stir in the Parmesan. Sprinkle the escarole with the Parmesan crumbs and serve.

SANJEEV KAPOOR

Indian-Style Mustard Greens

chef way

» *According to superstar Indian chef Sanjeev Kapoor, cooks in northern India make this dish, called* sarson ka saag, *when winter greens are in season. Traditionally, they cook the greens for up to an hour, stirring and pounding them with a large wooden muddler until a smooth paste forms.*

easy way

» *The greens—either peppery mustard greens or pleasantly bitter broccoli rabe—are wilted for just a few minutes, drained, then pureed in a food processor.*

INGREDIENTS 4 to 6 servings

1¼ pounds mustard greens, stemmed, or broccoli rabe, trimmed and chopped
½ pound cleaned spinach
2 tablespoons cornmeal
6 garlic cloves, chopped
4 jalapeños, seeded and finely chopped
One 2-inch piece of fresh ginger, peeled and chopped
2 red onions, finely chopped
¼ cup vegetable oil
Salt

TOTAL 35 minutes

1 Bring a large pot of salted water to a boil. Add the mustard greens and cook for 2 minutes. Add the spinach and cook for 30 seconds. Drain the greens, transfer to a food processor and puree. Sprinkle the cornmeal over the greens and pulse briefly to combine. Transfer the pureed greens to a bowl.

2 Add the garlic, jalapeños and ginger to the food processor and finely chop. Add the onions and finely chop.

3 In a large nonstick skillet, heat the oil. Add the garlic-onion mixture and cook over moderate heat, stirring occasionally, until lightly browned, about 7 minutes. Add the pureed greens and cook for 4 minutes, stirring occasionally; add about ¼ cup of water if the greens look dry. Season with salt and serve.

SERVE WITH Naan or *makki ki roti* (cornmeal bread).

VIKRAM SUNDERAM

Fresh Vegetable Curry

chef way

» *Vikram Sunderam of Rasika in Washington, DC, blanches his carrots, squash and green beans separately before cooking them in a deeply spiced curry sauce.*

easy way

» *The vegetables cook just once, right in the sweet and spicy sauce.*

INGREDIENTS 4 to 6 servings

- 2 tablespoons canola oil
- 1 small onion, thinly sliced
- 2 tablespoons finely julienned fresh ginger (from a 2-inch piece)
- 1 jalapeño, seeded and cut into thin strips
- 2 bay leaves
- 3 garlic cloves, minced
- 1 teaspoon turmeric
- 2 small tomatoes, coarsely chopped
- One 14-ounce can unsweetened coconut milk
- ¼ cup water
- Kosher salt
- 3 carrots, quartered lengthwise and cut into 1-inch pieces
- 1 pound butternut squash (neck only), peeled and cut into 1-by-½-inch pieces (1½ cups)
- ½ pound thin green beans, cut into 1-inch pieces
- Basmati rice, for serving

ACTIVE 20 minutes   **TOTAL** 1 hour

1 In a large, deep skillet, heat the oil. Add the onion, ginger, jalapeño and bay leaves and cook over moderate heat until softened, 5 minutes. Add the garlic and turmeric and cook, stirring, for 2 minutes. Add the tomatoes and mash lightly until just beginning to soften, 2 minutes. Add the coconut milk and water; season with salt. Bring to a boil.

2 Add the carrots, cover and simmer over low heat until crisp-tender, about 12 minutes. Add the squash and beans, cover and simmer until tender, about 15 minutes longer. Discard the bay leaves. Serve the curry with basmati rice.

WINE *Lime-inflected Austrian Grüner Veltliner: 2009 Weingut Bründlmayer Kamptaler Terrassen.*

JONATHON SAWYER

Farro with Artichokes

AND HERB SALAD

chef way

» *When he makes this farro dish at Cleveland's Greenhouse Tavern, Jonathon Sawyer poaches the artichokes in white wine, then uses the leftover artichoke poaching liquid to cook the farro.*

easy way

» *Trimming and poaching fresh artichokes is laborious; jarred marinated ones make quick work of this recipe.*

» *The farro simmers in store-bought chicken broth.*

INGREDIENTS 5 to 6 servings

- 4 tablespoons unsalted butter
- 1 carrot, finely diced
- 1 small celery root, peeled and finely diced
- 1 small onion, finely diced
- 2 celery ribs—1 finely diced and 1 thinly sliced, plus ½ cup celery leaves
- 1 bay leaf
- 2 cups farro (14 ounces)
- 1 cup dry white wine
- 4 cups low-sodium chicken broth

- Salt and freshly ground pepper
- 3 tablespoons grated Grana Padano cheese, plus shaved cheese for garnish
- 4 ounces marinated baby artichokes, drained and halved (¾ cup)
- ½ cup flat-leaf parsley leaves
- ¼ cup snipped chives
- 1 tablespoon tarragon leaves
- 1 teaspoon white wine vinegar
- 1 tablespoon extra-virgin olive oil

TOTAL 1 hour

1 In a large saucepan, melt 2 tablespoons of the butter. Add the carrot, celery root, onion, diced celery and bay leaf and cook over moderate heat, stirring occasionally, until the vegetables are lightly browned, about 5 minutes. Add the farro and cook, stirring, for 2 minutes. Add the wine and cook, stirring occasionally, until completely absorbed, about 5 minutes. Add half of the broth and cook, stirring occasionally, until completely absorbed, about 12 minutes. Season with salt and pepper. Add the remaining broth and cook, stirring occasionally, until completely absorbed, about 12 minutes longer. Discard the bay leaf. Stir in the grated cheese along with the artichokes and the remaining 2 tablespoons of butter until creamy. Spoon into bowls.

2 In a medium bowl, toss the sliced celery and celery leaves with the parsley, chives and tarragon. Add the vinegar and oil, season with salt and pepper and toss. Mound the salad over the farro, garnish with cheese shavings and serve.

MAKE AHEAD The recipe can be prepared through Step 1 and refrigerated overnight. Reheat before proceeding.

ANA SORTUN

Zucchini Stuffed with Shrimp & Feta

chef way

» *Ana Sortun of Oleana, a Middle Eastern–influenced restaurant in Cambridge, Massachusetts, tops her shrimp-stuffed zucchini with a tangy sauce of feta cheese, olive oil and Hungarian peppers (spicy wax chiles).*

easy way

» *Red bell pepper and crushed red pepper spice up the stuffing, eliminating the need for the Hungarian-pepper sauce.*

» *The roasted stuffed zucchini are topped with a little feta, then broiled.*

INGREDIENTS 6 servings

- 2 tablespoons extra-virgin olive oil, plus more for brushing
- 1 large white onion, finely chopped
- 1 red bell pepper, finely chopped
- ½ fennel bulb, finely chopped
- 1 large garlic clove, minced
- 4 plum tomatoes, chopped
- ½ teaspoon crushed red pepper

- Salt and freshly ground black pepper
- ¾ pound shelled and deveined large shrimp, finely chopped
- 2 tablespoons chopped parsley
- 2 tablespoons chopped dill
- 6 small, round or oblong zucchini (2½ pounds), halved lengthwise
- 1½ cups crumbled feta (6 ounces)

ACTIVE 40 minutes   **TOTAL** 1 hour 15 minutes

1 Preheat the oven to 425°. In a skillet, heat the 2 tablespoons of oil. Add the onion, bell pepper, fennel and garlic and cook over moderately high heat, stirring, until tender, 6 minutes. Add the tomatoes and crushed red pepper and cook, mashing, until thickened, 5 minutes. Season with salt and black pepper. Remove from the heat; let cool slightly. Stir in the shrimp, parsley and dill.

2 Using a spoon, scoop out the flesh of the zucchini, leaving a ¼-inch shell all around. Rub with oil. Season the zucchini shells with salt and pepper and stuff with the filling. Transfer to a lightly oiled roasting pan and roast for 30 minutes, until the filling is cooked through and the zucchini is just tender.

3 Preheat the broiler and position a rack 6 inches from the heat. Top the stuffed zucchini with the feta and broil for about 5 minutes, until the feta is melted and golden. Serve the stuffed zucchini hot or at room temperature.

WINE *Vibrant, berry-scented rosé: 2010 Domaine Houchart.*

JULIE ROBLES

Squash Gratin with Poblanos
AND SOUR CREAM

chef way

» *At Suzanne Goin and Caroline Styne's Tavern in L.A., chef Julie Robles makes this creamy, pepper-spiked gratin in individual dishes with a topping of candied pepitas (pumpkin seeds).*

easy way

» *Making one large gratin is much easier than preparing individual servings for each diner.*

» *Home cooks can use plain toasted pumpkin seeds instead of candied ones.*

INGREDIENTS 12 servings

- 6 large poblanos (about 1½ pounds)
- 2 large butternut squash (4 pounds total)—peeled, halved, seeded and sliced ½ inch thick
- ½ cup plus 1 tablespoon extra-virgin olive oil
- 1½ teaspoons coarsely chopped thyme
- Salt and freshly ground black pepper
- 1 large white onion, thinly sliced
- 3 large garlic cloves, thinly sliced
- 1 teaspoon coarsely chopped oregano
- ½ cup heavy cream
- ¾ cup crème fraîche or sour cream
- 8 ounces Monterey Jack cheese, shredded
- 8 ounces farmer cheese (see Note)
- Toasted pumpkin seeds, for serving

ACTIVE 45 minutes **TOTAL** 2 hours

1 Preheat the oven to 400°. Roast the poblanos directly over a gas flame or under the broiler, turning, until charred all over. Transfer the chiles to a bowl, cover tightly with plastic wrap and let cool. Peel, stem and seed the chiles, then cut them into thin strips.

2 Brush the butternut squash with 6 tablespoons of the olive oil and spread it on 2 large rimmed baking sheets. Sprinkle with 1 teaspoon of the thyme and season with salt and pepper. Roast for about 25 minutes, until the squash is tender, shifting the pans from top to bottom and front to back halfway through baking. Increase the oven temperature to 425°.

3 Meanwhile, in a large, deep skillet, heat the remaining 3 tablespoons of oil. Add the onion, garlic, oregano and the remaining ½ teaspoon of thyme; cook over moderate heat, stirring occasionally, until the onion is softened, about 8 minutes. Add the poblanos; cook until very tender, about 5 minutes. Add the heavy cream and simmer until thickened, about 5 minutes. Remove from the heat. Stir in the crème fraîche; season with salt and pepper.

4 Spoon half of the poblano mixture into a large baking dish and top with half of the butternut squash and half of the Monterey Jack and farmer cheeses. Repeat with the remaining poblano mixture, squash and both cheeses. Bake in the center of the oven for about 30 minutes, until the gratin is golden and bubbling. Let the gratin rest for 10 minutes. Garnish with the pumpkin seeds and serve.

NOTE Farmer cheese is a form of cottage cheese that has had the liquid pressed out. It's slightly tangy, with a dry texture that makes it great for crumbling. Look for it at specialty stores or cheese shops.
MAKE AHEAD The unbaked gratin can be refrigerated overnight. Return to room temperature before baking.

WINE *Fresh, melony Chenin Blanc: 2009 MAN Vintners.*

Desserts

BREANNE VARELA
Strawberry Scones
WITH ALMONDS

chef way

» *Pastry chef Breanne Varela of L.A.'s Tavern mixes frangipane (a rich almond paste) into the dough for her strawberry scones, which she makes for the restaurant's laid-back café and take-out spot, The Larder.*

easy way

» *These delicate scones get their almond flavor from a superfast buttermilk glaze that includes pure almond extract, a baking staple, instead of frangipane.*

INGREDIENTS Makes 16 scones

SCONES
1½ cups all-purpose flour
1½ cups whole wheat pastry flour
¼ cup plus 2 tablespoons granulated sugar
1 tablespoon baking powder
½ teaspoon baking soda
½ teaspoon salt
1 stick cold unsalted butter, cubed
1¼ cups buttermilk, plus more for brushing

1½ cups sliced strawberries
2 tablespoons turbinado sugar (also called Sugar in the Raw)

TOPPING
½ cup sliced almonds
2 cups confectioners' sugar
3 tablespoons buttermilk
½ teaspoon pure almond extract
Pinch of salt

ACTIVE 30 minutes **TOTAL** 1 hour 45 minutes

1 **MAKE THE SCONES** Preheat the oven to 400° and line 2 baking sheets with parchment paper. In a large bowl, combine the all-purpose and whole wheat pastry flours with the granulated sugar, baking powder, baking soda and salt. Using a pastry blender or 2 knives, cut in the butter until the mixture resembles coarse meal. Stir in the 1¼ cups of buttermilk and carefully fold in the strawberries.

2 Using an ice cream scoop or a spoon, scoop the dough into 16 mounds on the prepared baking sheets. Brush the scones with buttermilk and sprinkle with the turbinado sugar. Bake in the upper and lower thirds of the oven for 30 to 35 minutes, until the scones are golden and cooked through; shift the pans from front to back and top to bottom halfway through baking. Let the scones cool on a rack for 30 minutes.

3 **MAKE THE TOPPING** Lower the oven temperature to 350°. Spread the almonds in a pie plate and toast for about 8 minutes, until golden. Meanwhile, in a small bowl, whisk the confectioners' sugar with the buttermilk, almond extract and salt. Cover and let the glaze stand at room temperature.

4 Drizzle the scones with the glaze, then top with the almonds, pressing to help them adhere. Let dry for 10 minutes, then serve.

MAKE AHEAD The scones can be made up to 6 hours ahead.

ZOE BEHRENS

Banana Tart with Caramel Sauce

chef way

» *While working at 1789 in Washington, DC, Zoe Behrens made this banana tart with her own puff pastry and served it with homemade ice cream and rum raisins in caramel sauce.*

easy way

» *Using good store-bought all-butter puff pastry for the tart base shaves hours off the recipe.*

» *The caramel sauce here takes just five minutes to make.*

INGREDIENTS 6 servings

- 14 ounces all-butter puff pastry, thawed in the refrigerator
- 1 large egg yolk mixed with 1½ tablespoons water
- 5 small, just-ripe bananas, halved lengthwise
- 1½ tablespoons fresh lemon juice
- ½ cup sugar
- 6 tablespoons unsalted butter
- ½ vanilla bean, split, seeds scraped
- 2 tablespoons water

Sweetened whipped cream or vanilla ice cream, for serving

ACTIVE 25 minutes   **TOTAL** 1 hour 40 minutes

1 Preheat the oven to 375°. Line a baking sheet with parchment paper. On a lightly floured surface, roll out the puff pastry to a rough 10-by-15-inch rectangle, then trim it to a neat 9-by-14-inch rectangle. Using a ruler, cut a ¾-inch-wide strip of dough from each side; you will have 2 long and 2 short strips. Transfer the rectangle to the prepared baking sheet and brush with the egg wash. Set the strips on each side to form a border, pressing firmly to help the dough adhere; brush the strips with the egg wash. Freeze the tart shell until chilled, about 10 minutes.

2 Prick the bottom of the tart shell all over with a fork. Bake in the lower third of the oven for about 40 minutes, until the shell is puffed and golden. Press down the center of the shell slightly. Increase the oven temperature to 425°.

3 Rub the bananas with the lemon juice. In a skillet, cook the sugar over moderate heat, stirring until melted. Cook without stirring until a medium-amber caramel forms, about 5 minutes. Remove from the heat; whisk in the butter, vanilla seeds and water. Add the bananas and gently turn to coat with the caramel. Arrange the bananas in the tart shell, cut side up, leaving most of the caramel in the skillet. Drizzle ¼ cup of the caramel over the bananas. Bake the tart for about 20 minutes, until the bananas are slightly tender. Let cool slightly, then serve with whipped cream or ice cream, passing the remaining caramel on the side.

GALE GAND

Not Your Usual Lemon Meringue Pie

chef way

» *In her signature take on lemon meringue pie—a standby at Chicago's Tru for years— Gale Gand forgoes a traditional crust for quick-baked sheets of sugared phyllo dough, which she layers with house-made lemon curd and a brown sugar meringue.*

easy way

» *Frozen phyllo dough from the supermarket and jarred lemon curd (available at Whole Foods and specialty stores) replace Gand's made-from-scratch versions.*

INGREDIENTS 6 servings

- 3 sheets of phyllo dough, plus more in case of tearing
- 4 tablespoons unsalted butter, melted
- 2 tablespoons granulated sugar
- 1 cup light brown sugar
- 5 large egg whites
- One 12-ounce jar lemon curd
- Raspberries, for garnish

TOTAL 1 hour

---

1 Preheat the oven to 350°. Cut 2 sheets of parchment paper to fit a large baking sheet. Place 1 sheet of the parchment on a work surface. Top with a sheet of phyllo and brush with the melted butter. Sprinkle 2 teaspoons of the granulated sugar over the phyllo. Repeat with 2 more sheets of phyllo so that you have a stack of 3 sugared sheets. Using a ruler, trim the phyllo to a 12-by-16-inch rectangle, then cut it into twelve 4-inch squares. Slide the parchment onto a baking sheet and top with the second sheet of parchment paper. Bake for 18 minutes, until the phyllo squares are golden and crisp. Let cool completely.

2 Preheat the broiler. Put the brown sugar in a food processor; pulse to break up any lumps. In the bowl of a standing electric mixer fitted with a whisk, beat the egg whites at medium-high speed until soft peaks form. Beat in the brown sugar at high speed, a few tablespoons at a time, until the whites are glossy, 2 to 3 minutes. Transfer the meringue to a pastry bag with a plain tip.

3 Spoon a dollop of lemon curd onto each phyllo square. Pipe a layer of meringue over the lemon curd (alternatively, you can spoon the meringue over the lemon curd). Broil 6 inches from the heat for 1 minute, or until lightly toasted. Set 6 phyllo squares on plates and top them with the remaining 6 squares. Garnish with raspberries and serve right away.

WINE *Lightly sweet, sparkling Moscato d'Asti: 2009 Michele Chiarlo Nivole.*

BREANNE VARELA

Apple Pie Sundaes

WITH CHEDDAR CRUST SHARDS

chef way

» *Breanne Varela presents this decadent dessert at L.A.'s Tavern as a parfait, layering homemade apple ice cream with apple confit, cheddar crust and crème fraîche–whipped cream.*

easy way

» *Serving the dessert as a sundae—the components are scooped into a bowl—is easier than carefully layering in parfait glasses.*

» *Apple puree folded into frozen vanilla yogurt is a smart alternative to Varela's apple ice cream.*

» *Quick sautéed apples substitute for the slow-cooked apple confit.*

INGREDIENTS 8 servings

CHEDDAR SHARDS
¾ cup all-purpose flour
Kosher salt
4 tablespoons cold unsalted butter
½ cup shredded sharp cheddar cheese
2½ tablespoons cold water
¼ teaspoon cider vinegar

SUNDAE
6 tablespoons unsalted butter

6 large apples, such as Pink Lady or Granny Smith—cored, peeled and thinly sliced
¼ cup plus 2 tablespoons granulated sugar
¼ cup plus 2 tablespoons light brown sugar
½ teaspoon cinnamon
⅛ teaspoon freshly grated nutmeg
Kosher salt
2 pints vanilla frozen yogurt

ACTIVE 50 minutes   **TOTAL** 2 hours

1 **MAKE THE CHEDDAR SHARDS** Preheat the oven to 350°. In a food processor, combine the flour with ¼ teaspoon of kosher salt. Coarsely grate the cold butter into the food processor. Pulse until the mixture resembles coarse meal. Add the shredded cheddar cheese and pulse twice. Add the cold water and cider vinegar and pulse just until the dough is evenly moistened. Turn the dough out onto a work surface and knead until it just comes together. Wrap the dough in plastic and refrigerate for at least 20 minutes, or until chilled.

2 Line a baking sheet with parchment paper. On a lightly floured surface, roll out the dough to a 9-inch square and transfer to the baking sheet. Bake for about 40 minutes, until golden. Let cool.

3 **MEANWHILE, PREPARE THE SUNDAE** In a large skillet, melt the butter. Add the apples and toss to coat. Add the granulated sugar, light brown sugar, cinnamon and nutmeg and season lightly with salt. Cook over moderately high heat, stirring frequently, until the apples are tender and translucent, about 15 minutes.

4 Add ½ cup of water to the skillet and bring to a boil. Remove from the heat. Transfer half of the apples to a blender or food processor and puree until smooth. Scrape the puree into a bowl and freeze until it is cold, about 30 minutes.

5 Soften the frozen yogurt slightly and transfer it to a large bowl. Fold in the cold apple puree and freeze until the frozen yogurt is firm, about 30 minutes.

6 Scoop the frozen yogurt into 8 bowls and top with the sautéed apples. Break the cheddar crust into large shards; serve with the sundaes.

MAKE AHEAD The yogurt can be frozen for up to 3 days. The sautéed apples can be refrigerated for 3 days; bring to room temperature before assembling. The cheddar crust can be stored in an airtight container for up to 3 days. Recrisp in a warm oven.

MICHELLE VERNIER

Lemony Semolina-Jam Cake

chef way

» *When she was the pastry chef at Wildwood in Portland, Oregon, Michelle Vernier used individual ring molds to bake her semolina cakes. She flavored the cakes with Meyer lemon juice, then served them with Meyer lemon frozen yogurt.*

easy way

» *Baking the cake in a single springform pan is simpler than using individual molds.*

» *Meyer lemons have a short growing season. Adding a little sugar to regular lemons is a good way to re-create the slightly sweet Meyer lemon flavor.*

INGREDIENTS Makes one 8-inch cake

PASTRY CREAM
- ⅔ cup half-and-half
- 2 large egg yolks
- 2 tablespoons sugar
- 1 teaspoon all-purpose flour
- 4 teaspoons cornstarch
- Pinch of salt
- 2 teaspoons unsalted butter, softened
- ½ teaspoon pure vanilla extract

CAKE
- 6 tablespoons unsalted butter, softened
- 1 teaspoon finely grated lemon zest
- 1½ tablespoons fresh lemon juice
- ¾ cup plus 2 tablespoons sugar
- ¾ cup cake flour
- ¼ cup semolina
- 1½ teaspoons baking powder
- ¼ teaspoon salt
- 4 large egg whites (½ cup)
- ¼ cup seedless raspberry preserves
- Confectioners' sugar, whipped cream and raspberries, for serving

ACTIVE 30 minutes   **TOTAL** 1 hour 45 minutes

1 **MAKE THE PASTRY CREAM** In a small saucepan, bring the half-and-half to a simmer. In a medium bowl, whisk the yolks, sugar, flour, cornstarch and salt. Whisk in the hot half-and-half. Return the mixture to the saucepan and cook over moderate heat, whisking constantly, until very thick, about 3 minutes. Whisk in the butter and vanilla. Scrape the pastry cream onto a large plate and let cool to room temperature, about 10 minutes.

2 **MAKE THE CAKE** Preheat the oven to 375°. Butter an 8-inch springform pan. In a medium bowl, whisk the pastry cream with the 6 tablespoons of butter until smooth. Whisk in the lemon zest and juice. Add ¼ cup plus 2 tablespoons of the sugar, the cake flour, semolina, baking powder and salt and whisk the batter until smooth.

3 In a clean bowl, using an electric mixer, beat the egg whites at medium speed until soft peaks form. Gradually beat in the remaining ½ cup of sugar at high speed until the whites are glossy and stiff. At low speed, beat one-fourth of the beaten whites into the batter, then fold in the rest with a rubber spatula until no streaks of white remain.

4 Scrape the batter into the prepared pan and bake in the lower third of the oven for about 40 minutes, until the cake is golden and a skewer inserted in the center comes out with a few moist crumbs attached. Let cool in the pan for 20 minutes, then remove the ring and base and transfer to a rack to cool completely.

5 Using a serrated knife, split the cake in half horizontally. Spread the preserves on the bottom layer and replace the top. Dust with confectioners' sugar and serve with whipped cream and raspberries.

MAKE AHEAD The cake can be kept in an airtight container at room temperature for up to 2 days.

JANE TSENG
Pumpkin Cheesecake
WITH BROWN-BUTTER PEARS

chef way

» *Jane Tseng of Caffe Muzio and Stivale in New York City combines two holiday staples—gingersnaps and pumpkin pie—in cheesecake form. To make the cheesecake, she uses the tangy, soft-ripened Italian cheese Robiolina and house-made gingersnap cookies.*

easy way

» *Cream cheese fills in for Robiolina, which is somewhat expensive and hard to find.*

» *Boxed gingersnaps are an easy alternative to homemade cookies.*

INGREDIENTS 10 to 12 servings

CHEESECAKE
- 8 ounces gingersnap cookies, crushed
- ⅔ cup plus 2 tablespoons sugar
- Salt
- 2 tablespoons unsalted butter, softened
- 12 ounces cream cheese, softened
- 1 cup canned pumpkin puree
- ½ teaspoon pure vanilla extract
- 2 large eggs
- ¼ cup all-purpose flour
- ⅛ teaspoon cinnamon
- Pinch of freshly grated nutmeg

PEARS
- 4 tablespoons unsalted butter
- 3 large, ripe Bartlett pears— peeled, cored and cut into thin wedges
- 1 teaspoon sugar

ACTIVE 45 minutes   **TOTAL** 2 hours + 4 hours chilling

1 **MAKE THE CHEESECAKE** Preheat the oven to 350°. In a food processor, pulse the gingersnaps with 2 tablespoons of the sugar and a pinch of salt until fine crumbs form; add the softened butter and process until moistened. Using your fingers, press the crumbs into the bottom of a buttered 9-inch springform pan in an even layer; brush any crumbs off the side of the pan. Bake the crust for about 10 minutes, until lightly browned. Let the crust cool slightly, then wrap the bottom of the pan tightly in aluminum foil so it's watertight. Set the pan in a large, deep skillet or a small roasting pan.

2 Rinse out the food processor bowl and wipe it dry. Add the cream cheese, pumpkin puree, vanilla and the remaining ⅔ cup of sugar and process for about 30 seconds, or until smooth. Add the eggs and pulse to blend. Add the flour, cinnamon, nutmeg and ½ teaspoon of salt and process for about 30 seconds, or until smooth. Carefully pour the filling over the crust. Set the skillet in the oven and carefully pour in enough hot water to reach halfway up the side of the springform pan. Bake the cheesecake for about 55 minutes, until barely jiggly in the center. Carefully transfer the skillet to a rack and let the cheesecake cool. Remove the foil and refrigerate the cheesecake until firm, at least 4 hours or overnight.

3 **PREPARE THE PEARS** In a large skillet, cook the butter over moderately high heat until lightly browned and nutty-smelling, about 3 minutes. Add the pears and cook, turning once, until softened and lightly browned, about 4 minutes. Add the sugar and cook, turning once, until the pears are glazed, about 1 minute.

4 Run a sharp knife around the edge of the cheesecake and remove the springform ring. Cut the pumpkin cheesecake into wedges and serve with the warm pears.

MAKE AHEAD The cheesecake can be refrigerated for up to 3 days.

WINE *Juicy, sweet white: 2008 Anam Cara Cellars Nicholas Estate Gewürztraminer from Oregon.*

MEGAN GARRELTS

Graham Cracker Pound Cake

chef way

» *Megan Garrelts creates clever desserts like this Graham Cracker Pound Cake at her restaurant Bluestem in Kansas City, Missouri. She serves the cake with sage-glazed figs and spiced walnut gelato.*

easy way

» *This cake comes together quickly with pantry staples. Omitting the figs and gelato makes it faster still.*

INGREDIENTS Makes one 8-by-4-inch loaf

- 1½ sticks unsalted butter, softened
- ½ cup granulated sugar
- ¼ cup dark brown sugar
- 1½ cups cake flour
- ½ cup finely ground graham cracker crumbs, from half a sleeve
- ¾ teaspoon baking powder
- ¼ teaspoon salt
- 3 tablespoons whole milk
- 2 tablespoons heavy cream
- 3 large eggs
- 1 tablespoon pure vanilla extract

ACTIVE 20 minutes **TOTAL** 1 hour 30 minutes

1 Preheat the oven to 325°. Spray an 8-by-4-inch glass loaf pan with vegetable oil spray. In a large bowl, using an electric mixer, cream the butter with the granulated sugar and dark brown sugar. In a medium bowl, whisk the cake flour with the graham cracker crumbs, baking powder and salt. In a small bowl, whisk together the whole milk, cream, eggs and vanilla. Beating at medium speed, add the dry and liquid ingredients to the butter mixture in 3 alternating batches.

2 Scrape the batter into the prepared loaf pan and bake in the lower third of the oven for about 55 minutes, until a toothpick inserted in the center comes out with a few moist crumbs attached. Let cool in the pan for 15 minutes, then turn the pound cake out onto a rack to cool completely.

MAKE AHEAD The cake can be kept in an airtight container for up to 3 days or frozen for 2 weeks.

KRISTIN FERGUSON

Pineapple Upside-Down Cake

chef way

» *Kristin Ferguson, the pastry chef at Forage in Los Angeles, prepares this Pineapple Upside-Down Cake as single servings. She pairs the mini cakes with homemade buttermilk ice cream.*

easy way

» *A full-size cake isn't as cute as Ferguson's miniature desserts, but using an 8-inch round pan means less prep time and less cleanup.*

» *Store-bought ice cream or whipped cream takes the place of homemade buttermilk ice cream.*

INGREDIENTS Makes one 8-inch cake

¾ cup plus 2 tablespoons light brown sugar
1½ sticks unsalted butter, softened
1 vanilla bean, split, seeds scraped
½ large pineapple—peeled, quartered, cored and sliced ⅓ inch thick
½ cup sour cream

2 large eggs
1 teaspoon pure vanilla extract
1¼ cups all-purpose flour
¾ cup granulated sugar
½ teaspoon baking powder
¼ teaspoon baking soda
½ teaspoon salt

ACTIVE 30 minutes **TOTAL** 1 hour 30 minutes

1 Preheat the oven to 350°. Butter an 8-inch round cake pan. Sprinkle the bottom with 2 tablespoons of the brown sugar.

2 In a large skillet, combine the remaining ¾ cup of brown sugar with the ½ stick of butter and the vanilla bean and seeds and cook over moderately low heat until the butter is melted. Add the pineapple and cook over moderately low heat, stirring occasionally, until tender, about 20 minutes. Using a slotted spoon, arrange the slices in the cake pan, overlapping them if necessary. Remove the vanilla bean and pour the pan juices over the pineapple.

3 In a bowl, whisk ¼ cup of the sour cream with the eggs and vanilla. In another bowl, beat the flour, granulated sugar, baking powder, baking soda and salt. Add the remaining stick of butter and ¼ cup of sour cream and beat at low speed until smooth, then beat at medium speed until fluffy. Add the sour cream–egg mixture and beat again until fluffy, 2 minutes.

4 Spoon the batter over the pineapple and spread it evenly. Bake for about 40 minutes, until the cake is deep golden. Let cool for 5 minutes on a rack. Run a knife around the edge of the cake, invert it onto a plate and remove the pan. Replace any pineapple that may have stuck to the pan. Serve warm or at room temperature.

SERVE WITH Vanilla ice cream or sweetened whipped cream.

BREANNE VARELA

Chocolate-Chip-Pecan Cookie Bars

chef way

» *Breanne Varela's chocolate chip cookies are hugely popular at L.A.'s Tavern, in part because each one is filled with big chocolate chunks.*

easy way

» *Bars are easier to prepare than individual cookies.*

» *These cookie bars are very versatile. Home cooks can swap walnuts or almonds for the pecans, or use half nuts and half dried cranberries for tart, chewy bars.*

INGREDIENTS Makes 32 bars

- 1 cup pecans
- 4 tablespoons unsalted butter, softened
- 2 tablespoons canola oil
- ¼ cup plus 2 tablespoons granulated sugar
- ¼ cup plus 2 tablespoons light brown sugar
- 1 large egg
- 1 teaspoon pure vanilla extract
- 1½ cups whole wheat pastry flour
- ½ teaspoon baking soda
- ½ teaspoon kosher salt
- 1 cup semisweet chocolate chips

ACTIVE 20 minutes **TOTAL** 1 hour

1 Preheat the oven to 350° and line the bottom of a 9-by-13-inch baking pan with parchment paper. Spread the pecans in a pie plate; toast for about 8 minutes, until golden. Chop the pecans; let cool.

2 In the bowl of a standing electric mixer, beat the butter and oil with the granulated sugar and brown sugar until creamy. Beat in the egg and vanilla until smooth. In a small bowl, whisk the flour with the baking soda and salt; beat the dry ingredients into the mixer at low speed. Add the chocolate chips and pecans; beat just until incorporated.

3 Transfer the dough to the prepared baking pan and press into an even layer. Bake for about 20 minutes, until lightly browned and nearly set in the center. Let cool completely, then run a knife around the edges and invert the rectangle. Peel off the paper and invert onto a cutting board. Cut and serve.

MAKE AHEAD The cookie bars can be stored in an airtight container at room temperature for up to 5 days.

KAREN HATFIELD

Devil's Food Cupcakes

WITH ESPRESSO MERINGUE

chef way

» *Karen Hatfield usually prepares mini versions of this recipe for the petit-four plate at her L.A. restaurant Hatfield's. She tops the chocolate cupcakes with a swirl of espresso meringue and cocoa-nib dust.*

easy way

» *Baking full-size cupcakes speeds up the process: There are fewer cupcakes to frost.*

» *Instead of ground cocoa nibs, a dusting of cocoa powder and instant espresso tops the frosted cupcakes.*

INGREDIENTS Makes 24 cupcakes

CUPCAKES
- 4 ounces unsweetened chocolate, finely chopped
- ¼ cup Dutch-process cocoa powder, plus more for sprinkling
- 1¼ cups boiling water
- 1½ cups all-purpose flour
- 1 teaspoon baking soda
- ¼ teaspoon salt
- 2 sticks unsalted butter (½ pound), softened
- 1½ cups packed dark brown sugar
- 3 large eggs
- ½ cup buttermilk
- 1 teaspoon pure vanilla extract

ESPRESSO MERINGUE
- 3 large egg whites
- 1½ cups confectioners' sugar
- 1 teaspoon instant espresso, plus more for sprinkling

ACTIVE 30 minutes **TOTAL** 1 hour

1 **MAKE THE CUPCAKES** Preheat the oven to 325°. Line 24 muffin cups with paper liners. Lightly spray the paper liners with vegetable oil spray. In a small bowl, mix the chocolate and ¼ cup of cocoa. Add the boiling water and let melt, then whisk until smooth. In a medium bowl, whisk the flour with the baking soda and salt. In a large bowl, using an electric mixer, beat the butter and brown sugar until fluffy. Beat in the eggs, buttermilk and vanilla, then slowly beat in the dry ingredients and the chocolate mixture in 3 alternating batches.

2 Fill the muffin cups three-fourths full with the batter. Bake for 22 to 25 minutes, shifting the pans halfway through, until the cupcakes are springy and a toothpick inserted in the center comes out with a few moist crumbs attached. Let the cupcakes cool in the pans for 15 minutes, then unmold them and transfer to a rack to cool completely.

3 **MEANWHILE, MAKE THE ESPRESSO MERINGUE** Mix the egg whites, confectioners' sugar and 1 teaspoon of instant espresso in a medium stainless steel bowl. Set the bowl over a saucepan of simmering water and heat the whites, whisking constantly, until hot to the touch (165°). Transfer the egg white mixture to the bowl of a standing electric mixer fitted with a whisk and beat at high speed until the meringue is stiff and glossy, about 5 minutes; if using a handheld mixer, beat for about 8 minutes.

4 Scoop half of the espresso meringue into a pastry bag fitted with a large (¾-inch) plain tip and pipe onto half of the cupcakes. Repeat with the remaining meringue and cupcakes. Lightly sprinkle the meringue with cocoa and instant espresso and serve.

MAKE AHEAD The frosted cupcakes can be kept in an airtight container overnight.

MAURA KILPATRICK

Chocolate-Hazelnut Baklava

chef way

» *At Ana Sortun's Oleana in Cambridge, Massachusetts, pastry chef Maura Kilpatrick intensifies the flavor of her baklava by soaking the dessert in a syrup infused with cocoa nibs and cinnamon.*

easy way

» *The baklava is fabulous even without the cocoa-and-cinnamon-spiked syrup. This recipe uses a simple 10-minute honey syrup.*

INGREDIENTS Makes 24 pieces

1 pound hazelnuts	1 pound phyllo dough
12 ounces bittersweet chocolate, coarsely chopped	2 sticks unsalted butter, melted
2⅔ cups sugar	2 cups water
1½ tablespoons cinnamon	1½ cups honey

ACTIVE 1 hour   **TOTAL** 2 hours 15 minutes + 4 hours cooling

1 Preheat the oven to 350°. Spread the nuts on a baking sheet and bake for 12 minutes, until the skins are blistered; let cool. Leave the oven on. Transfer the nuts to a kitchen towel and rub off the skins, then transfer to a food processor and pulse until coarsely chopped.

2 Add the chocolate, ⅔ cup of the sugar and the cinnamon to the food processor and pulse until the chocolate and nuts are finely chopped and the same size.

3 Unwrap the phyllo and cover with a sheet of plastic wrap. Generously butter a 9-by-13-inch metal baking pan. Butter and stack 8 sheets of phyllo. Trim the edges. Ease the stack into the pan. Sprinkle about 2 cups of the filling over the phyllo. Butter and stack 2 more phyllo sheets; fold them in half crosswise and place over the filling. Sprinkle on another 2 cups of the filling. Top with 2 more buttered, folded sheets and 2 cups of filling. Butter and stack 3 more phyllo sheets, fold them in half and place over the filling. Fold in the overhanging phyllo on top and brush generously with butter. Using a ruler and a sharp knife, cut the baklava (through the top and bottom) into 3-inch squares (there will be a bit left on one long side). Cut each square in half to make triangles.

4 Bake the baklava for 25 minutes, then lower the oven temperature to 300° and bake for 50 minutes longer, until golden.

5 In a saucepan, bring the water, honey and the remaining 2 cups of sugar to a boil. Simmer over moderate heat for 10 minutes. Immediately ladle the hot syrup over the hot baklava and let stand until completely cool, at least 4 hours and preferably overnight.

MAKE AHEAD The baklava can be covered with foil and kept at room temperature for up to 2 days.

CHRIS BROBERG

Deep, Dark Chocolate Pudding

chef way

» *This pudding was one component of an elaborate seven-part dessert at Café Gray (now closed) in New York City, where Chris Broberg (currently the pastry chef at New York's Four Seasons Restaurant) served it in a chocolate-coffee tuile.*

easy way

» *There's no need for all the other sweets. This lush, intensely chocolaty, easy-to-make pudding is terrific served on its own.*

INGREDIENTS Makes 3½ cups (6 servings)

- 5 ounces bittersweet chocolate, chopped
- 2 tablespoons unsalted butter
- 2⅓ cups whole milk
- ½ cup sugar
- Pinch of salt
- 2 tablespoons Dutch-process cocoa powder
- 1 tablespoon cornstarch
- 2 large egg yolks, plus 1 large egg
- 2 teaspoons pure vanilla extract
- 1½ teaspoons instant espresso
- Lightly sweetened whipped cream, for serving

TOTAL 30 minutes + 4 hours chilling

1 Set a fine strainer in a bowl over a larger bowl of ice water. Microwave the chocolate and butter until melted. Let cool slightly.

2 In a medium saucepan, simmer 2 cups of the milk with ¼ cup of the sugar and the salt. In a small bowl, whisk the cocoa powder and cornstarch with the remaining ⅓ cup of milk. Whisk the cocoa paste into the hot milk. In the same bowl, whisk the yolks and whole egg with the remaining ¼ cup of sugar. Gradually whisk some of the hot milk mixture into the eggs to warm them, then whisk the egg mixture into the saucepan and cook over moderately high heat, whisking, until very thick, about 5 minutes. Remove from the heat and whisk in the chocolate-butter mixture, vanilla extract and instant espresso. Strain the pudding into the bowl set in the ice bath and stir until cooled. Place a sheet of plastic wrap directly on the surface of the pudding and refrigerate until chilled, at least 4 hours or overnight. Serve with whipped cream.

Contributors

josé andrés is the chef and co-owner of several restaurants around Washington, DC, including Jaleo, Minibar by José Andrés and Zaytinya, as well as the Bazaar by José Andrés at SLS Hotel in Beverly Hills and China Poblano and Jaleo in Las Vegas. He is also the culinary director and partner of SLS Hotel. *thinkfoodgroup.com*

eric banh and his sister, **sophie banh,** own the modern Vietnamese restaurants Monsoon in Seattle and Monsoon East in Bellevue, Washington, as well as the newly opened Ba Bar noodle shop in Seattle. Eric also owns the Seattle-based Baguette Box sandwich shops. *monsoonrestaurants.com*

lidia bastianich is the chef and co-owner of Felidia in New York City and Lidia's Italy in Pittsburgh and Kansas City, Missouri, and a co-owner of Eataly, a market and restaurant complex in New York. She is also the host of the PBS series *Lidia's Italy* and the author of several cookbooks, including *Lidia Cooks from the Heart of Italy. lidiasitaly.com*

mario batali is the chef and co-owner of over a dozen restaurants in New York City, Las Vegas, L.A. and Singapore, among them Manhattan's Babbo, Lupa and Esca, as well as a co-owner of Eataly, a market and restaurant complex in New York. He has authored several cookbooks, most recently *Molto Gusto,* and stars on Food Network's *Iron Chef America.* He also hosts *The Chew,* a new daytime talk show on ABC. *mariobatali.com*

rick bayless, an F&W Best New Chef 1988, is the chef and owner of Frontera Grill, Topolobampo and Xoco, all in Chicago, and the founder of Frontera Foods. He is also the host of the PBS series *Mexico—One Plate at a Time.* His most recent cookbook is *Fiesta at Rick's. rickbayless.com*

zoe behrens was the pastry chef at 1789 Restaurant in Washington, DC.

daniel boulud, an F&W Best New Chef 1988, is the chef and owner of New York City's Daniel, Café Boulud, DB Bistro Moderne, Bar Boulud, DBGB Kitchen and Bar, Boulud Sud and Épicerie Boulud, with spin-offs around the world, including Bar Boulud in London and Maison Boulud in Beijing. The author of several cookbooks, he has most recently co-authored *Braise: A Journey Through International Cuisine. danielnyc.com*

chris broberg is the pastry chef at the Four Seasons Restaurant in New York City. *fourseasonsrestaurant.com*

andrew carmellini, an F&W Best New Chef 2000, is the chef and co-owner of Locanda Verde and The Dutch, both in New York City. He is also a co-author of two cookbooks: *Urban Italian* and *American Flavor. andrewcarmellini.com*

ratha chaupoly is the co-chef and co-owner of the Num Pang Sandwich Shops in New York City. *numpangnyc.com*

tom colicchio, an F&W Best New Chef 1991, is the chef and owner of Craft, Craftbar, Craftsteak and 'wichcraft, with locations throughout the country. He is also the head judge on Bravo's *Top Chef* and author of three cookbooks: *Think Like a Chef, Craft of Cooking* and, most recently, *'wichcraft. craftrestaurant.com*

chris cosentino is the chef at Incanto in San Francisco, the author of the website Offalgood.com and co-creator of Boccalone, an online artisanal salumeria. *offalgood.com*

kristin ferguson is the pastry chef at Forage and a pastry and baking instructor at Ecole de Cuisine, both in Los Angeles. *foragela.com*

bobby flay is the chef and owner of several restaurants in the US and Bahamas, including Mesa Grill and Bar Americain in New York City and Bobby's Burger Palace, with various East Coast locations. A star of Food Network's *Grill It!, Throwdown!* and *Iron Chef America,* he has also written many cookbooks. His newest, *Bobby Flay's Bar Americain Cookbook,* will be published in fall 2011. *bobbyflay.com*

jason franey, an F&W Best New Chef 2011, is the chef at Canlis in Seattle. *canlis.com*

gale gand, an F&W Best New Chef 1994, is the pastry chef and co-owner of Tru in Chicago and the author of several cookbooks, including *Gale Gand's Brunch!* and *Chocolate and Vanilla. galegand.com*

jose garces is the chef and owner of several Philadelphia restaurants, including Amada and Tinto, and Chicago's Mercat a la Planxa. He is also the author of *Latin Evolution. grg-mgmt.com*

megan garrelts is the pastry chef and co-owner of Bluestem in Kansas City, Missouri. She also co-authored *Bluestem, The Cookbook,* which will be published in fall 2011. *bluestemkc.com*

trina hahnemann is a chef, food writer and cookbook author based in Copenhagen. Her most recent book is *The Nordic Diet. trinahahnemann.com*

ryan hardy was the chef at Montagna in the Little Nell hotel in Aspen, Colorado.

karen hatfield is the pastry chef and co-owner of Hatfield's in Los Angeles. *hatfieldsrestaurant.com*

dionicio jimenez is the chef at El Rey in Philadelphia. *elreyrestaurant.com*

sanjeev kapoor is an international celebrity chef based in India, where he has a daily cooking show. He has more than 20 restaurants and 140 cookbooks to his name. His most recent cookbook, *How to Cook Indian,* is his first published in America. *sanjeevkapoor.com*

maura kilpatrick is the pastry chef at Oleana in Cambridge, Massachusetts.

mourad lahlou is the chef and owner of Aziza in San Francisco. His first cookbook, *Mourad: New Moroccan,* will be published in fall 2011. *aziza-sf.com*

corey lee is the chef and owner of Benu in San Francisco. *benusf.com*

donald link is the chef and owner of Herbsaint and co-chef and co-owner of Cochon and Cochon Butcher, all in New Orleans. He is also the co-author of *Real Cajun: Rustic Home Cooking from Donald Link's Louisiana. donaldlink.com*

pino maffeo, an F&W Best New Chef 2006, was the chef at the former Restaurant L in Boston.

nobu matsuhisa, an F&W Best New Chef 1989, is the chef and co-owner of Nobu and Matsuhisa restaurants around the world and author of *Nobu: The Cookbook. nobumatsuhisa.com*

shawn mcclain is the chef and owner of Green Zebra in Chicago and chef and co-owner of Sage in Las Vegas. *greenzebrachicago.com*

george mendes, an F&W Best New Chef 2011, is the chef and owner of Aldea in New York City. *georgemendesnyc.com*

charles phan is the chef and owner of the Slanted Door, Out the Door and Heaven's Dog and a co-chef and co-owner of Academy Café, all in San Francisco. *charlesphan.com*

wolfgang puck is the chef behind L.A.'s Spago and co-owns a dining empire. He has also authored eight cookbooks and hosted and appeared on several TV programs, including Food Network's *Wolfgang Puck. wolfgangpuck.com*

richard reddington is the chef and co-owner of Redd in Yountville, California. *reddnapavalley.com*

lulzim rexhepi was the chef at Kittichai in New York City.

akasha richmond is the chef and owner of Akasha in Culver City, California, and the author of *Hollywood Dish. akasharestaurant.com*

julie robles is the chef de cuisine at Tavern in Los Angeles. *tavernla.com*

jonathon sawyer, an F&W Best New Chef 2010, is the chef and owner of the Greenhouse Tavern in Cleveland. *thegreenhousetavern.com*

bruce sherman, an F&W Best New Chef 2003, is the chef and co-owner of North Pond in Chicago. *northpondrestaurant.com*

ana sortun is the chef and owner of Oleana restaurant and chef and co-owner of Sofra bakery and café, both in Cambridge, Massachusetts. She is also the author of *Spice. oleanarestaurant.com*

mark sullivan, an F&W Best New Chef 2002, is the chef and co-owner of Spruce in San Francisco and the Village Pub in Woodside, California. *sprucesf.com*

vikram sunderam is the chef at Rasika in Washington, DC. *rasikarestaurant.com*

jerry traunfeld is the chef and owner of Poppy in Seattle and author of *The Herbal Kitchen. poppyseattle.com*

jane tseng is the pastry chef at Caffe Muzio, Stivale and Spasso, all in New York City. *caffemuzio.com*

breanne varela is the pastry chef at Tavern and the Larder at Tavern in Los Angeles. *tavernla.com*

michelle vernier was the pastry chef at Wildwood Restaurant in Portland, Oregon.

michael white is the chef and owner of Marea, Osteria Morini and Ai Fiori restaurants in New York City. *marea-nyc.com*

takashi yagihashi, an F&W Best New Chef 2000, is the owner of Takashi and Noodles by Takashi Yagihashi, both in Chicago. He is also the co-author of *Takashi's Noodles. takashichicago.com*

Index

PHOTOGRAPHERS

quentin bacon 35, 45, 63, 85, 115, 161, 177, 229

james baigrie 57, 135, 167

joseph de leo 17, 23, 29, 203

stephanie foley 27, 51, 73, 81, 105, 113, 147, 169

frances janisch 25, 65, 103, 143

david malosh 6, 19, 55, 121, 123, 173, 181, 193, 205, 213, 217

kana okada 31, 49, 93, 141, 219, 245

con poulos 53, 157, 185, 221, 225, 231, 235, 241

tina rupp 11, 15, 21, 33, 37, 41, 43, 47, 59, 67, 69, 75, 77, 79, 87, 89, 91, 95, 99, 107, 111, 117, 119, 125, 127, 129, 131, 145, 149, 163, 165, 189, 199, 211, 215, 227, 233, 239, 243, 247

lucy schaeffer 13, 97, 101, 137, 139, 151, 153, 155, 171, 175, 179, 183, 191, 195, 201, 207, 209, 237

anson smart 71, 187

FOOD&WINE
BOOKS

More books from
FOOD&WINE

Annual Cookbook
Over 700 recipes from the world's best cooks—including celebrity chefs and cookbook authors like Jean-Georges Vongerichten, Paula Wolfert, Tyler Florence and Eric Ripert.

Best of the Best Cookbook Recipes
More than 100 tantalizing recipes from the best cookbooks of the year, chosen by FOOD & WINE. Authors include Alice Waters, Emeril Lagasse, Jamie Oliver and Giada De Laurentiis.

Cocktails
Over 150 stellar drink and snack recipes from the most acclaimed mixologists and chefs, plus an indispensable guide to cocktail basics (essential spirits, key glassware and tools) and the top bars and lounges around the country.

Wine Guide
The most up-to-date guide, with over 1,000 recommendations and an easy-to-use food pairing tip sheet.

TO ORDER, CALL 800-284-4145
OR LOG ON TO **foodandwine.com/books**